6 **DAY** PUBLISH

TURN YOUR IDEA INTO A PUBLISHED BOOK IN 6 DAYS, OR LESS

BOGDAN JUNCEWICZ

AUTHOR OF SKILLED SUCCESS

www.BogdanJuncewicz.com
ISBN-10: 1539602796
ISBN-13: 978-1539602798

TABLE OF CONTENTS

Preface: It's Impossible! (This Isn't A Book You Read) 1

Section 1: The Thousand Year Old Marketing Tool   8

Chapter 1: It's More Than Just A Book 9
Chapter 2: What The Heck Does A 17 Year Old Kid Know
About Publishing, Teaching & Sharing A Message? 13

**Section 2: Are these myths holding you back? (Do this
instead)   18**

Chapter 3: The Slow & Steady Myth 19
Chapter 4: The Perfection Myth 31
Chapter 5: The Jump Straight In Myth 36

Section 3: The 6 Day Publish Process   38

Chapter 6: The 6 Day Publish Checklist 39

Section 4: Stage 1: Prepare   48

Chapter 7: Know Thy Market 49

Section 5: Stage 2: Pre-Work   69

Chapter 8: Your Publishing Blueprint 70
Chapter 9: Analysis 74
Chapter 10: Purpose 88
Chapter 11: Strategy 95

Section 6: Stage 3: Present   100

Chapter 12: Creating A Killer Book Brand 101
Chapter 13: Your Writing Game Plan 122
Chapter 14: Creating Your Audience-Captivating Design
.... 158

Section 7: Stage 4: Produce   170

Chapter 15: Writing Is The Secret 171
Chapter 16: Writing Hacks 173

Section 8: Stage 5: Publish   178

Chapter 17: The Finish Line 179

Section 9: The Next Steps   182

Chapter 18: You're Not Alone 183
Chapter 19: The Final Puzzle Piece 189

Dedication 199

The 6 Day Publish Checklist 200

PREFACE: IT'S IMPOSSIBLE! (THIS ISN'T A BOOK YOU READ)

It's just NOT possible.

An idea into a published book in 6 days; that's crazy.

That's what some people think to themselves when they hear about this book.

Not you, though.

You asked yourself a very different question.

A question that changes everything.

You may have asked yourself..

'What if it was… what if it was possible to turn my idea into a published book in 6 days, or less?'

That's why I want to thank, and congratulate, you for taking the right first step and getting your hands on a copy of this book.

So, you have an idea, and you're here to learn how to turn that idea into a published book in 6 days, or less.

Great… you're in the right place.

But, if you don't have an idea yet… then you're in the wrong place (for now at least).

If you don't have a book idea yet, and you want one, then this will be the best place for you to start (it's all free):

FindingYourIdea.6DayPublish.com

Awesome.

Imagine if just 6 days after you finish reading this book, you could be a published author..

..and imagine yourself reaping all of the rewards that come with that title… published author.

..multiplied credibility… huge income potential… a marketing tool that can bring you more business than you can ever dream of.

Now, I have a question for you..

Do you realize how, now, you are hooked?..

..you started reading this preface and now with every line..

..with every single line..

..you get more and more hooked into the contents of this book.

Reading these words, you think to yourself that you should stop reading these words just to prove me wrong..

..but you don't.

You just keep reading.

Word by word.

Line by line.

Now, I'm not saying this to put you in some kind of hypnotic trance.

I'm saying these words, because isn't that what you want your readers to feel like when they read your book?

You do want your readers to be hooked into your stories, your content, and your book, when it's published, don't you?

Realize how I said 'when' and now 'if'..

'WHEN your book gets published!'

So, how can I be so certain?

2 reasons actually.

1. I believe in you. The fact that you are reading this book, reading these words, shows me you are an action taker. And, it's the action takers that get the results in this world (we both already know that though).

2. I believe in the content of this book. This book is crafted to share with you **everything** you need to know to get your book written, and published, in 6 days, or less.

Hence, this book is NOT a book you read.

It's a book you DO.

In fact, it's more of a manual, or a workbook, than it is a book.

What it really is though, is a **_proven step-by-step process_** for turning any idea into a published book in 6 days, or less.

If you're reading this book, odds are, you have a message, a story to share, or a difference to make. And, odds are, you want to build greater credibility, multiply your income and impact lives on this planet.

This book will give you all of that (and more!)

Now, you may be thinking..

'Bogdan, do you really believe this book will change my life?'

As much as I would love to give you a **BIG THUMPING YES** response..

..the answer is NO.

This book will not change your life.

This book, **_PLUS your action and implementation_**, _though_, WILL change your life forever.

No doubt about it.

The content and guidance I share, applied, will get you the results you want.

Hands down.

(I know that may sound kinda arrogant... and don't get me wrong, it is… but what you are about to discover just flat out works.)

The question is..

Are you ready to… learn the secrets to turning your idea into a fully-written, published book in 6 days, or less?

I know you have many choices as to how you can spend your time.

No doubt about it.

Some people.. some books.. some content gets your attention.

Most of it probably doesn't.

I need your attention.

I need you to be committed right now and give me your attention for the length of this book.

You gave me your hard-earned money for this book. Whether it's the book price or just the shipping cost.

Either way, you gave me your hard-earned money.

Allow me to, in return, give you 100X that amount in value (minimum!)

Unfortunately, though, I can only do so much... you need to actually read the contents of this book and implement.

Commit to reading this book for at least 15 minutes per day.

And if you're a high achiever, more than that.

This way you will truly get the life-changing value from this book.

I will support you to get your book published so that people, on this planet, can hear your message.

I've got your back, but I need you to stick with the game plan.

Sound fair enough?

Great.

For the longest time, people have been attempting to sabotage and limit our potential.

The education system, the media, the governments have been limiting our potential for as long as we can remember.

They have been telling us what's possible, and what isn't, **without** any real proof.

What you will discover in this book is so-called unconventional wisdom.

This book is not about speculation, it's not about guesswork.

The book-writing process you will discover in this book is not based on theory, it's based on testing.

I have personally tested it all out.

My first book took 6 days to publish (yes, from idea to publish in 6 days;) hence the name of this book.

And yes, you guessed it, I am applying the same 6 Day Publish Process to get this book written and published.

The only difference is that this time, I have given myself only 4 days to get this book written and published.

I might fail *(oh well.. I guess I will have to just live with the failure).*

It's a challenge.

Anyway, it's 9:18am as I write these words to you.

It's the 18th of October 2016. Day 1 of 4.

I have been working on the pre-work, prep and writing of these words since 6am this morning. *(I'll share more about this later)*

Anyhoo..

..you have an idea, a story or content people on this incredible planet needs to hear..

..so without further ado, let's get started.

Turning your idea into a published book in 6 days, or less; go to the next page, and let the journey begin.

SECTION 1:

THE THOUSAND YEAR OLD
MARKETING TOOL

CHAPTER 1: IT'S MORE THAN JUST A BOOK

'Not everything is as seems'

Those are the word's of the guru from the Karate Kid movie, and they can't be more true.

You see, a book is more than just a book.

A book is the ultimate thousand-year-old marketing tool for building a brand, building a business and sharing your message.

For thousands of years, people have written, and read, books as sources of wisdom and guidance.

Also, a book is the ultimate positioning tool that allows you to position yourself as an authority, and as an expert, in your industry.

A book is the key to the gateway of endless possibilities.

Imagine for a moment that you are a school teacher..

Now, think about how much you would earn as that school teacher.

$30 per hour...maybe $50 per hour.

And as a school teacher, you would probably work 7, 8, maybe 9, hours a day to make a living.

And every day, you would have to work to get paid.

The school you work at wouldn't just keep paying you if you left and stopped working there permanently.

But, what if they did?

Imagine it for a moment..

..you go and teach some students at a school some stuff… let's say over the course of a week..

..and what if… what if the school actually paid you, every month, for the rest of your life for the teaching you did that week…

Imagine if it were possible for a moment..

..how awesome would that be if it were possible?

And I especially love this part; being the deliverer of good news..

IT IS POSSIBLE! (and it's easier than you think to achieve)

The missing piece in the puzzle (the answer) is your book.

You write a book and get it published, over the course of 6 days, and now, you can use that work, the book, to earn money for the rest of your life.

You don't have to re-write the book every time you make money from it.

You don't have to rewrite the book for every copy you sell.

That would just be plain stupid *(and terribly ineffective!)*

You see, when you write, and publish, your book, you join the elite group of people that make money, and make an impact, while they sleep, while they lay on the beach, or while they do whatever they want.

However, chances are, this isn't the first time you have heard that writing a book is a great idea.

You've probably been told about the importance of getting your book written and published countless times before.

However, there have probably been many reasons that may have held you back in the past..

..reasons that have stopped you from getting your book written and published, fast!

That's ok.

I've been there. It took me 6 months of procrastination to even get started on my first book.

With one of the main reasons being, I didn't have a system... I didn't have a structured process to follow... and I was just left in a state of permanent confusion.

Then, once I got started, the book was published in 6 days.

You see, the challenges… the obstacles… the excuses, that have held you back in the past DON'T MATTER.

Once you start writing your book, most of those excuses will vanish anyway.

Poof.

Gone.

Either way, you have **everything** you need *right now* to get your book written.

If you have just 2 things… an idea, and the willingness to turn that idea into a book… you're packed and ready for the journey ahead.

Let me support you with the rest; with everything else.

Let the proven system you are about to discover, the system that turns ideas into published books in 6 days, or less.. let that system support you with everything else.

Your message, your story, your content, it deserves to be heard..

..and I can practically guarantee someone on this planet needs it more than you can ever even imagine right now.

Now's the time. Now's your time.

Let's continue, shall we?

CHAPTER 2: WHAT THE HECK DOES A 17 YEAR OLD KID KNOW ABOUT PUBLISHING, TEACHING & SHARING A MESSAGE?

There I was..

..about 4 years ago..

..it was like any other day..

..yet, with one slight difference.

It was the last day of the school year before the summer holidays.

I left school and went home expecting nothing different than any other day.

Then, I received confirmation on a big request I made to my parents.

Let me rewind a bit..

A few months prior, after months and months of deliberation, I made a choice. I made a choice together with my parents..

I wanted to leave school and become home-schooled. Self-taught.

(Looking back at it now, that decision made a huge difference in my life, and it kinda makes me wonder why I didn't have the courage to make that decision earlier)

Anyway, back to the last day of the school year..

I received confirmation from my parents (Business owners) that this was, in fact, the very last day that I had ever stepped into a school as a student.

I was 14 years old.

I was excited..

..yet very nervous at the same time.

I was excited because this freed up an extra 7-8 hours a day for me to study what I really thought was important.

Yet I was nervous because this upped the ante, it turned up the pressure..

And the other decision I made that day was that I was not going to study the normal school curriculum, meaning that I essentially made the choice to become a 'voluntary high-school dropout,' with no schooling certificates, no hopes of university and no chances of college.

I did this to pursue my dreams, my dreams of starting a business, sharing my message, changing the world, being free and living life on my terms - this was the exciting part.

The part that made me nervous at the time was the fact that I no longer had a plan B.

In other words, if I failed on my chosen journey of business and entrepreneurship, I couldn't go back and just get a job because NOBODY would hire me.

(I wouldn't even qualify to work at McDonald's)

I was either going to succeed on this new journey or I was totally screwed.

With this rather positive reassurance, I started to take action *:p*

I started studying.

I started learning life skills. Business skills.

I was determined. Committed to reaching my goals.

I started my first digital marketing & digital advertising business when I was 15.

You see, while other kids were playing video games, I was creating content, building out sales processes and making money while I sleep.

Let's fast forward a bit to 2016..

Over the last 5 years, I have learned with, learned from, and most importantly, taught thousands and thousands of students all around the world. Everywhere from Australia to the UK, from India to Singapore and other places in between.

I wrote my first book, *Skilled Success*, in 6 days, that year.

To summarize... I'm a 2 time published author, an international speaker who has travelled all around the world teaching thousands and thousands of students in just the last 12 months, and CEO of 2 businesses.

To call those last few lines shameless self-promotion is a frickin' understatement.

Here's the thing, though..

When most people look at me, or any other 17 year old, their first thought isn't *'author, international speaker & CEO,'* their first thought is usually *'I wonder how many hours a day this kid spends partying it up & playing video games'*

In other words, I hope you can forgive and overlook my shameless self-promotion because the value you will receive from this book may just change your life.

Now, this book is not about getting your book written and published..

..it's about getting it written and published *in 6 days, or less.*

You must know that the process... the system... is very different for getting your book written and published *fast.*

That's why in the next section, we are going to identify the key myths... the key obstacles... that could get in your way.

An army doesn't go into battle unprepared… of course not… they carefully identify where the enemies will most likely be so they can be prepared.

The same applies here.

If you know what might stop you from getting your book written and published in 6 days, or less..

..you will be prepared to overcome those obstacles and achieve the outcome you want.

That's all jam packed into the next section.

The very next section..

SECTION 2:

ARE THESE MYTHS HOLDING YOU BACK? (DO THIS INSTEAD)

CHAPTER 3: THE SLOW & STEADY MYTH

In school, you were probably told the old fable about the Tortoise and the Hare..

Here's a quick, shortened version..

The tortoise, fed up at being ridiculed for his slowness, challenges a boastful hare to a race. The hare jumps out to an early lead and then gets cocky. He takes a nap. When he wakes up, the tortoise has crossed the finish line and won.

But here's the weird part.. most people will tell you that the lesson of that story is *'slow and steady wins the race.'*

Huh? Come again?

That makes no sense whatsoever.

How many races (Formula 1, NASCAR, 100m athletic sprint, cycling, rally racing, swimming) have you ever seen where 'slow and steady' won?

Absolutely zero, right?

Slow and steady loses the race. Every frickin' time.

Here's the methodology we should actually follow *(the one that gets really gets results)*:

Success Loves Speed

Yet, the myth is that, if you want to achieve something, like write a book, *slow and steady* will get the best results.

It's total B.S.

In fact, if you write a book in 6 days, the quality of that book, in most cases, will actually be better, not worse, than if you wrote that book in 3 months.

You may think.. *'Why?'*

Well, when you work in a state of immersion… in a state of complete focus, you're not distracted..

..and everybody knows that it's when we are focused that we do our best work.

No matter whether it's a painter, a writer, a singer, etc, their best work is done when they are focused.

In other words, most people's understanding of how to write a high quality, engaging and informative book, effectively and efficiently, is… how do I put this nicely?

Flawed.

Yes, very flawed. It's not your fault though..

Chances are, you have been misled by the education system, by marketers, and by the so-called guru's that writing a book takes months of preparation, and is a long, difficult and very time-consuming process.

These people have either knowingly, or unknowingly, misled you to believe something that just isn't true; they didn't tell you the real secrets to getting your book written effectively, to a high standard, so that you can use it to get the results you want!

(That way they can keep selling you more stuff as you keep struggling)

And it pisses me off! Big time.

Don't get me wrong..

..you may have started your book, and you may have even made some good progress over the last few weeks, and months, with it.

You may have gotten your first book *(and maybe even consecutive ones)* published (congratulations **:)**)

However, no matter what publishing stage you are at, I can almost guarantee that if you're reading these words, you have been held back from the real juicy and effective publishing results.

(The life-changing results that, deep down, you truly desire)

Here's probably what you were misled to believe:

1. Block out 15 - 30 minutes every day over the next few weeks (and maybe even months) to write.

2. Commit to writing 150 - 300 words per day.

3. And eventually, in a few months (maybe years) you will complete your book, and get it published.

150 - 300 words per day? Seriously?

If you're anything like me, you probably don't want to wait many months (and maybe even years) until your book is finally completed and published.

People on this incredible planet are struggling from problems that **YOU** know how to fix..

They are hanging from the edge of a cliff *(a metaphorical cliff that is)* attempting to pull themselves back up to safety..

..but they can't (without support).

They need your help. They need your message, your story, your content to inspire, uplift and educate them.

You hold the answers that can help people all around the world live better, happier and more successful lives.

They are hanging from that cliff attempting to save themselves.

Give them a helping hand… help pull them up to greater results.

Your book can do that.

The question is..

..do you want to give them a helping hand as soon as you can, or a few months/years from now.

Remember, ***success loves speed.***

Don't get me wrong... the *slow and steady* approach... it does work sometimes.

'Well, Bogdan, why mess with something that isn't broken?

If you don't want to, you don't have to.

You can just keep attempting to write your book the same way *(the average, often ineffective, way)*

Nothing wrong with that.

As I said, it sometimes works.

However, as Albert Einstein said so perfectly:

'The definition of insanity is doing the same thing over and over again, but expecting different results'

Are you happy with your publishing results?

I mean, REALLY HAPPY?

What if you could discover a way that gets much better results (2, 5 and even 10 times faster as well)..

And I mean much, MUCH better results.

The improved model that I'm gonna reveal to you is only for people who want better results..

..for those who want more..

..it's for people who don't want to work on their book for months (and maybe even years) before they reap any rewards.

It's for people that rather invest a few days (6 days, or less) and start reaping rewards straight away.

(Frankly, if I had to work for many months to get this book published, I would have just stopped and worked on something else, and you wouldn't be reading these words.)

Fortunately, you can take advantage of *The 6 Day Publish Process* and get your book published in just 6 days *(or even less!)*

The core of how, and why, *The 6 Day Publish Process* can get you such incredible results, in such a short period of time, is a concept called **immersion.**

Let me share a quick story that I shared in *Skilled Success* to demonstrate the power of immersion.

We arrived.

We didn't know what to expect.

We were here seeking abundance and prosperity.

My parents made one huge life decision, with little preparation.

Let me rewind a bit.

I was born in Gdansk, Poland, and I, and my brother, were raised by our parents in Poland for the first few years of our lives.

My dad was running a successful furniture business in Poland for many years..

..however, my parents aren't the type of people who settle for good.

(One of the many things I admire about them)

So one day their ambition encouraged them to make a decision.

A decision that changed our lives forever..

We weren't fully prepared but we just went for it, having faith.

My parents decided to close everything down, pack it all up and move.

We moved from Poland to the city where so many people move to in search of abundance.

We arrived here.

We didn't know the culture. We didn't know what to expect.

We didn't even know the language.

We hadn't had a single lesson of the English language in our entire lives.

(FYI, we moved to London, England)

I, and my brother, started going to school.

My parents started a construction business.

We all struggled our way through the first few months, slowly learning the language so that we could actually communicate with other people.

We continued struggling through it, knowing we had no other choice.

Fortunately, we started getting somewhere.

If we really wanted to live and work in the lands of abundance, whether it's the UK, or the US, Canada, Australia, Singapore, or whatever country it is..

..we needed to know their language to communicate.

Then, after a few months, we started picking up more and more of the language.

In fact, in just a few years (if not less), my English was completely fluent.

In fact, after just a few years of living in London, and communicating in English all the time, my English was far better than my birth language of Polish.

This story demonstrates the power of **immersion.**

If we lived in Poland and just took English language lessons, it would have taken us 2, 3, 4, maybe even 5 times longer to learn fluent English.

And that's not even exaggerated.

Statistics show that it takes many, many more years to become fluent in a new language through study.

Through **immersion**, me, my family, and probably tens, and hundreds, of thousands of people around the world have been able to skip years of study to achieve the same desired result.

Immersion helps accelerate learning, skill development, results, and more specifically in the context of this book, it accelerates the process of turning your idea into a published book, fast.

Here's what immersion in the context of book writing looks like..

It's currently 15:18. I just checked into a hotel, in which I will stay for the next 3 nights (4 days).

I just started an *hour-long focus block (I'll share about this later)*

Immersion is a state of complete focus on a given activity.

Here's the challenge for you... if you are serious about turning your idea into a published book in 6 days or less..

..go to your schedule/calendar and find a 6-day block of time (6 days back-to-back) and block those 6 days out to get your book written.

Don't worry about 'how' you will get the book written in 6 days or less, I'll share about this in upcoming sections..

..what's important right now is that you take that 6-day block of time and block it out.

If you can't find a 6-day block of time within the next few weeks/months, simply find 3 different 2-day blocks of time, and block those out.

This isn't ideal, but it will work.

YOUR 6 DAY PUBLISH BLOCK:

Write the dates in here… during which 6 days are you going to write your book *(schedule 6 days in... if it takes less than 6 days, only then add something else)*

(Example) Day 1 of 6: <u>18/10/2016</u>
(Example) Day 2 of 6: <u>19/10/2016</u>

```
Day 1 of 6: __/__/____
Day 2 of 6: __/__/____
Day 3 of 6: __/__/____
Day 4 of 6: __/__/____
Day 5 of 6: __/__/____
Day 6 of 6: __/__/____
```

Now, I need you to understand that those 6 days are now sacred.

Don't schedule any meetings, any phone calls, or anything else during those 6 days.

During those 6 days, the goal is for you to focus completely on writing your book (and nothing else).

Here's why:

If you distracted, you actually lose IQ points.

In fact, a recent study shows that when you are just multi-tasking, it's like you just lost 10% of your IQ.

If 10% doesn't sound like a lot, let me give you a comparison.

That same study shows that when someone is stoned they lose only 5% of their IQ points.

Yes, when you're distracted, multitasking, you are essentially stoned out of your mind.

Actually, it's like you're stoned twice, that's the impact of distraction.

Hence, if the only change you make is your prioritization of '**focus**', that will radically improve your results.

Immersion taps into this power of focus for maximization of your potential.

That's why as we speak, I am in a hotel room. Alone. Focused.

Now, I love people. You probably do too.

It's not the easiest thing to lock yourself in a hotel room and be completely uncontactable for 6 days. I get it.

If you can't do that… do the next best thing… and attempt to get as close to that as possible.

That's immersion, and it's only when you are completely 100% focused, immersed… no facebook… no social media… no cat videos… that you become optimally productive.

So, if you haven't already, go up and block out 6 days to get your book written.

What you might not know *(and this may just pleasantly surprise you)* is that..

..a book only takes about 35 - 45 hours to write.

That's 35 - 45 focused hours.

And as I have banged on about in this chapter, focused hours (immersion) are very different than the average working hours.

Here's the ideal time-structure to write your book.

6 days.

6 - 10 hour-long focus blocks per day.

And *voila*… at the end of that time, if you follow the system laid out in this book, you will have a published book.

So, what exactly do I mean by *'hour-long focus blocks?'*

I mean, 1-hour-long periods of time when you are 100% focused on your book work.

What this looks like for me is simple..

1-hour block of time… timer set… headphones on… focused.. ignore everything around me… phone off… no social media… no distractions… no interaction with others (unless this is part of the task)... doing NOTHING else other than focused work.

Now, after you complete each hour-long focus block, you want to stand up, stretch, relax, whatever you want, before going into the next focus block.

Here's why..

..in just 2 or 3 hour-long focus blocks, you will get more done than most people get done between the hours of 9am and 5pm.

Test it, you'll see.

And this is how you want to write your entire book; 6 days, with each day consisting of 6 - 10 of these hour-long focus blocks.

That's the method of maximum productivity *(and most effective results!)*

In the next chapter, we are going to, together, conquer the myth that holds back not just authors, but speakers, business owners, and product developers, all around the world from the success they want to achieve.

CHAPTER 4: THE PERFECTION MYTH

Perfection; it's a mirage.

If there is one main thing that stops people from getting their books started, written, and published, it's this..

The perfection myth.

The myth that *'if you put enough work, and enough time, into it, eventually it will be perfect, and you can finally publish it'*

It's a complete myth *(yet it limits so many people)*.

Most people publish their books far too late.

Did you know that Apple launched the iPhone without the copy and paste function (and without many other semi-important functions)?

You may think… *'That's stupid.'*

Well.. not exactly.

You see, Steve Jobs, he knew that if he took the time to add the copy and paste function *(and all of the other missing functions)* he would miss out on the opportunity that the phone market provided at the time.

In other words, instead of seeking perfection, Steve Jobs, launched the iPhone earlier than the competition launched their smartphones, and by doing this, secured large market share in the phone market.

Then, once he got his product out here, **and only then**, did he update and improve it.

If he waited… waited until the phone was 'so-called perfect,' then frankly, we would still be waiting for the iPhone launch.

He would have missed out on that golden opportunity and would have had to pay the price for it.

So, here's how you publish your book *(the 6 Day Publish way)*:

You proof it, make it 85% perfect.. then you publish it.

You start building buzz around the book, you start making sales, you start promoting it, and then, **and only then**, you go back and update the book with changes to make it ever better.

I read the book, *Lean Startup*, a while back, and it changed my entire perspective when it comes to product development.

Your book is your product, and therefore it requires the best, and most effective, product development strategy; this book is that strategy.

Like it or not, whenever we are writing books, we are guessing..

We are guessing what our audience's will want to hear, what our audience's will respond to, and what our audiences will value.

And yes, with thorough market research, we can remove a lot of the guesswork..

..but not all of it.

The way to remove ALL of the guesswork is to actually become your customer.

Maybe in the future, you will be able to actually become other people... I mean like, step into their identities *(not sure how I feel about this)*, but right now, the technology just isn't there...

So, what is the closest, and best, way to get the most accurate data about what your potential customers will want, will respond to and will value in your book?

The answer... **customer feedback.**

ASK.

Ask them what they want, will respond to, and will value in your book.

Let's say that you are with a friend at a shopping mall.

You could spend all day guessing, researching and putting together weird experiments to examine what your friend feels like eating for lunch today..

..yes, she ate this yesterday... and this last week... and this last year on this day, that means she must want to eat this for lunch.

..or you could simply put an opinion out there and ask..

'Hey, wanna eat Chinese for lunch? How about Italian? What do you feel like eating?'

And that's what you want to do with your book.

Stop guessing what your audience will respond to.

Instead get your book written, get it published, and ask your audience..

'Thanks for reading the book. What did you like the most about it?'

What other questions to you have about ABC topic, that I didn't answer in the book?

What would you have liked to see more of in the book?

What didn't you like about the book?

What else?

What else would you have liked to see shared in the book?

These are all questions that you should ask your audience after you write your book.

Anyway, the book, *Lean Startup*, go buy it and read it *(if you haven't already)*

Back to *the perfection myth*.

Don't critique what you write.

And no matter what you do, do not edit while you write.

Don't you dare do that! *:)*

Just write.

Some people write a chapter.. then spend 4 months editing it.

Don't.

Pretend your laptop doesn't have a 'backspace/delete key.

Write your entire book, start to finish, and only then, edit *(we'll talk about this in later sections of this book).*

To summarize, the goal with your book, just like with any information product, and just like the most successful marketers, and billion dollar companies have been doing for decades, is to launch your book, fast.

Get it out there... get sales... gain proof of concept... get customer feedback... go back, improve the book... re-release it... and repeat this cycle.

Here's the lesson:

Good Enough Is Good Enough

Don't worry about making your book perfect right away.

Get your book written and get it published, fast.

Then you can focus on tweaking, improving and reaching perfection.

Got it? :)

CHAPTER 5: THE JUMP STRAIGHT IN MYTH

Creativity is a fascinating thing.

If you have read about the last 2 myths, you may be thinking to yourself..

'Well, Bogdan, the best way must be to simply jump straight in and start writing straight away'

Now, this myth (#3) is on the complete other side of the scale from *the perfection myth*, yet this myth is equally as detrimental.

You see, planning is important.

Very important in fact.

It's important to writing, it's important to publishing, and it's important to creativity.

The challenge many people have is over-planning, and never actually getting started.

It's all about balance, it's a dance.

A lot of what you will learn in this book is about planning your book.

Here's the thing, if you plan your book correctly, the writing process will become 5, and even 10X easier.

Let's go back to the point of…

'This is not a book you read' for a moment (this is important)

As I have said before, this is a book you DO..

..and that's why, in this book, there are exercises for you to complete.

Each exercise is in this book for a specific purpose, and if you follow through, and complete all of the exercises, you will actually make more progress during the length of this book then some people make in a few months of planning their book.

Don't take my word for it though… you'll see for yourself.

By this point, pretty much all the foundations for getting your book written, and published in 6 days, or less, have been laid.

From this point forward in the book, we are going to dig into the actually 6 Day Publish Process and start working on **your** book.

It's an exciting journey we are going to embark on together..

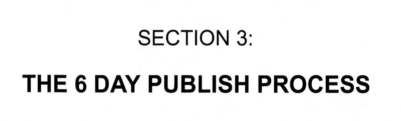

SECTION 3:

THE 6 DAY PUBLISH PROCESS

CHAPTER 6: THE 6 DAY PUBLISH CHECKLIST

It's a checklist… a proven… *do this, then this, then complete this…*style checklist for getting your book written and published.

One of the main reasons people fail to get their books written, and published, is this..

They focus on *'getting it published'* from the very beginning.

You may be thinking..

'Wait… what... Bogdan, what's wrong with that?'

Let me explain..

You see, there is nothing wrong with that goal *(in fact, that what's expected)*..

..the challenge with that is that most people have the *'publish book'* goal..

..however, they lack the '*stepping stone*' goals to get there.

And frankly, they get overwhelmed.

And quit.

Let me give you this example:

Before I wrote my first book, I spend about 6 months, or so, committing and de-committing... continually procrastinating to get started on my book.

Here's why..

During those 6 months, I was only focused on the '*publish book*' goal.

Then after about 6 months, I changed my approach.

I started **bite-sizing.**

Meaning, I still focused on the big goal (a published book), but I also had smaller, bite-sized goals (stepping stones) that I focused on.

I created stepping stones to that goal and focused on achieving those.

Step by step.

Section by section.

Chapter by chapter.

And I started making rapid progress on the book.

My first book was written in 6 days.

And btw… it's day 2 of 4 for me right now writing this book that you are reading.

I love the quote by Will Smith:

"You don't set out to build a wall. You don't say 'I'm going to build the biggest, baddest, greatest wall that's ever been built.' You don't start there. You say, 'I'm going to lay this brick as perfectly as a brick can be laid. You do that every single day. And soon you have a wall."

That's what this 6 Day Publish Process *(and this 6 Day Publish Checklist)* is all about.

Bite-sizing.

Step by step progress.. *(and it works!)*

You start laying those bricks (completing steps on the checklist)... step by step..

..and before you know it.. you have the biggest, baddest, greatest wall that's ever been built *(a published book that flat out rocks!)*

The 6 Day Publish Checklist consists of 5 stages:

- PREPARE
- PRE-WORK
- PRESENT
- PRODUCE
- PUBLISH

Each stage is crucial to the overview publishing process…

Anyway, without further ado, here's the checklist:

BOOK CREATION & PUBLISH CHECKLIST

DOCUMENT	COMPLETE?

PREPARE

- READ & SUMMARIZE 5 SIMILAR BOOKS
- SUMMARIZE 5 MOST SIMILAR COURSES/EVENTS/VIDEOS
- WRITE LIST OF EVERYTHING I ALREADY KNOW ON GIVEN TOPIC
- RESEARCH COMPETITION

PRE-WORK

- MARKET PROBLEM ANALYSIS
- BUYER CUSTOMER AVATAR
- DIFFERENTIATION FACTOR ANALYSIS
- DISRUPTIVE IDEA ANALYSIS
- BUYING HOOK ANALYSIS

- EDUCATIONAL PURPOSE
- COMMERCIAL PURPOSE

- MARKETING & PROFIT STRATEGY ANALYSIS
- PUBLISHING STRATEGY

PRESENT

- BOOK TITLE
- BOOK SUBTITLE/S
- COLOUR PREFERENCES AND ANALYSIS
- AUTHOR + AUTHOR CREDITS

- SECTION OVERVIEW (Usually 3-9)
- SECTION CHAPTER OVERVIEW (Usually 10 - 30)
- CHAPTER KEY POINT OVERVIEW (Usually 3-8/chapter)
- SECTION BRANDING
- CHAPTER BRANDING

- FRONT COVER DESIGN
- BACK COVER DESIGN
- SPINE DESIGN
- FINALIZED PRINT-READY DESIGN

PRODUCE

- INTERIOR TITLE PAGE
- COPYRIGHT NOTICE (OPTIONAL)
- DEDICATION (OPTIONAL)
- ACKNOWLEDGEMENTS (OPTIONAL)
- TABLE OF CONTENTS
- SECTION #1 WRITTEN
- SECTION #2 WRITTEN
- SECTION #3 WRITTEN
- SECTION #4 WRITTEN
- SECTION #5 WRITTEN
- SECTION #6 WRITTEN
- SECTION #7 WRITTEN
- SECTION #8 WRITTEN
- SECTION #9 WRITTEN

- BASIC BOOK FORMATING CHECK (SPELL, GRAMMAR CHECK)
- TITLES, TABLE OF CONTENTS, SECTIONS & CHAPTERS FORMAT
- JUSTIFICATION & CENTRALIZATION FORMAT
- BOLD/ITALICS/UNDERLINE FORMAT
- FORMAT KEY SOUNDBITES TO STAND OUT
- FINALIZED PRINT-READY PDF

PUBLISH

- REVIEW/BOOK PROOFING
- RETAIL PRICING
- HIT **'PUBLISH'**

(there's also a copy of this checklist at the back of the book so you can actually fill it out while you're completing your book)

Also, if you want a digital copy, a spreadsheet version or a version you can print out, of this checklist… simply go to:

FreeBonuses.6DayPublish.com

Anyway, let's go through it.

Let's break down the 5 core stages of the 6 Day Publish Process.

STAGE 1: PREPARE

The better, the more rigorous, your preparation is, the easier your book will be to write.

This stage consists of you actually researching your competition, researching your market and finding valuable data that will help you, not just write your book, but make it a huge success.

STAGE 2: PRE-WORK

Some people want to skip the pre-work, they want to skip the preparation and jump straight into it.

How do I know that?

Well… because I'm one of those people..

Hence, just like I tell myself, I'm going to tell you..

STOP IT! DON'T!

The more work you put in during the pre-work stage, the easier your book writing, and book publishing, process will be.

It's as simple as that.

STAGE 3: PRESENT

This stage consists of..

..branding your book, branding your book sections, and chapters, designing eye-catching and captivating covers to present your content in, and a whole lot more.

STAGE 4: PRODUCE

Now we get into the nitty-gritty part, the juicy part of the process *(a.k.a. the hard work)*.

Now, if you've done the first 3 stages properly *(don't worry, I've got your back)*, then this stage will actually be far easier than you may think.

Most people think to themselves..

'Wait, I've got to write 150 - 250 pages of content, what the heck am I going to write? What if I run out of stuff to write; what if I get writer's block?'

All valid concerns.

Don't worry, you're not the only one. I asked myself all of those questions before.

I don't worry about this stuff anymore, and here's why..

If you put in the hard work during the **pre-work**, and during the **present**, stages, these so-called writing challenges won't be so challenging for you any longer.

I need you to trust the process.

Think Karate Kid.

The kid didn't know the way ahead, but he trusts the process, and he got the results that he wants.

Trust The Process

And that brings us onto stage 5..

STAGE 5: PUBLISH

This stage is the good part… the fun part.

It's also the easy part.

It's the part that's the most rewarding.

Imagine, hitting publishing, and seeing your book available for people to order and read.

This stage, stage 5, is the goal.

And it's your obligation to get to this stage and get your book published.

Yes, your obligation.

Here's the thing, if you have a message to share, that will help people overcome challenges and gain greater levels of success in life, it's your obligation to get your book out there and get it read.

People deserve to hear your message, to hear your story, and to be inspired by your work.

Publishing your book is the ultimate win-win situation.

Your audience wins. The publisher's win.

And you win because, your book, positioned effectively, can give you an endless amount of opportunities for fame, fortune and freedom.

Ok, so, by now in this book, you know that getting your book published is vitally important, for you, and for the world.

You know the myths that limit so many people.

And you know that through *immersion*, and by following a proven step-by-step system, you can avoid falling victim to those myths.

Rather, by following the process you are about to discover, you know that you will get far greater results, in a far shorter period of time.

Now, over the next 5 sections, I will go into the details of the 6 Day Publish Process, through each of the 5 stages, so that, by the end, you will have total clarity regarding the steps you need to take to get your book, written and published.

The journey continues…

SECTION 4:

STAGE 1: PREPARE

CHAPTER 7: KNOW THY MARKET

Have you ever been at a party, at a meeting, or just hanging out with some friends, when someone calls a cab.. then they ask you..

'Where are you heading?'

You tell them where you are heading.

They say, *'Hey, I'm heading in that direction too, want to share a cab/taxi?'*

You say, *'Well, as long as you're already going that way..'*

Now, as long as this person isn't an axe murder, this makes perfect sense.

Why take two cabs instead of one, right?

This concept may seem simple, but it's really powerful.

Allow me to explain..

You probably don't deliver your own parcels.

You either use the postal service, FedEx, UPS or some other major delivery service, right?

In fact, every merchant who ships products does the same thing.

Pretty much nobody delivers their own packages.

Because FedEx, USPS, and UPS are already going that way.

Those delivery services have the infrastructure in place.

They have planes that are already flying that way. Drivers who are already driving that way.

The incremental cost of adding YOUR package to their route is almost ZERO.

That's because they're already going that way.

But to deliver that package yourself would cost you hundreds of dollars (renting a delivery vehicle, hiring a driver, plane tickets, the cost of your time, etc.)

It would be crazy for you to fly to a certain country just to deliver a package.

And this applies to almost everything: you don't make your own clothes, you don't build your own house, you don't grow your own food…because someone else already has a system in place that is far more efficient.

Now you may be thinking..

'Cool story Bogdan, but what does this have to do with your writing & publishing a book?'

Well… a lot actually.

A lot of people that attempt to write and publish their book attempt to create it from the ground up. From scratch.

They attempt to figure out, on their own, what their audience will want.

They attempt to figure out, on their own, what titles, what contents, what design, what everything, will give them the best publishing results.

They attempt to figure everything out on their own.

Trial and error.

Attempting to create something (a book) from the ground up.

It makes no sense.

Alternatively, imagine if you could discover exactly what your market wants, needs and buys, before you even write a word of your book..

That's what this first part of The 6 Day Publish Process is all about; *preparation*.

Now, imagine this… imagine completing your book..

Publishing your book..

Launching your book..

..and crickets.

Nothing. You make little-to-no sales and get little-to-no results.

Now, this example is not designed to put you off from the idea of writing a book.

Far from it.

One of the biggest fears of writing, publishing and launching a book is publishing a book that nobody wants.

It's a real concern.

I get it.

What this stage; *prepare*, will help you do is avoid that through strategic market research.

Just like the 'shipping your own parcels' example, trial and error is not the way to go when publishing a book.

Instead, *strategic market research IS the way to go.*

Stop attempting to create your book infrastructure from scratch and start leveraging existing data to deliver your message.

Let's dig in.

Here's the PREPARE part of the 6 Day Publish Checklist:

PREPARE
- READ & SUMMARIZE 5 SIMILAR BOOKS
- SUMMARIZE 5 MOST SIMILAR COURSES/EVENTS/VIDEOS
- WRITE LIST OF EVERYTHING I ALREADY KNOW ON GIVEN TOPIC
- RESEARCH COMPETITION

If you complete these 4 steps you will have a far greater understanding of what your market wants than pretty much most other authors in your market.

Why?

Because most people don't do the research.

Now, as I said before, the temptation is for you to want to just skip this stage.

'I know my market already. I know what they want'

I can't even recall how many times I have told myself that, then motivated myself to go and do even more market research, only to find hidden gems of information that I didn't yet know.

Don't skip this stage.

This stage is like the foundations of a building. If that building was built on weak foundations, under pressure, it would collapse.

The same applies to your book foundations.

What keeps your market, your potential book customers, up at night?

What are their fears?

What do they really want?

What has been missing from the information they have read before on your topic?

The more research you do, the better you will be able to communicate your message to your audience.

And the best way to learn about what influences your audience is to see what your audience is already being influenced by.

So, how can you find out what your audience is already influenced by?

Here are 4 proven ways:

#1) READ & SUMMARIZE THE 5 MOST SIMILAR BOOKS

If someone has bought a book similar to yours, clearly that book was successful at marketing and positioning itself for that target customer.

Now, this is step is semi-optional.

You don't have to read 5 books as part of this process… the value comes from 'summarizing' and 'examining' why these 5 books are selling well.

So, right now, go to Amazon.com, or any other book site you choose, and find the 5 most similar, and successful books (books that sell well), for your niche and write down those 5 book titles.

---

5 SIMILAR BOOKS TO LEARN FROM:

1. _____
2. _____
3. _____
4. _____
5. _____

Yes, stop reading this book for the moment, go to an online bookstore..

..find 5 similar books that you can learn from, and model, and write them down in the box above.

This may seem extremely easy.. and it is.. but what's easy to do, is also easy not to do.

As I said before, this isn't a book you read.

It's a book you DO.

And, you will learn far more from trusting the process, and going through these exercises, than from any other book publishing course you could possibly buy.

Now, order these 5 books, or buy the digital Kindle versions of these books (optional)

If you don't want to buy the books, not recommended, simply bookmark these book pages.

You can learn a lot about these books from the title, the reviews and from the previews alone.

Next, review these books, and think about the learnings.

If you did the last exercise as specified, the 5 books you picked are books that are selling well.

Meaning, those 5 books are resonating with the target market well.

Now, what can you learn about message delivery, cover design and book branding from these books?

What benefits are these books appealing to?

What makes people want to buy these books?

What do these books do, that you can do with your book, to get similar (and even better!) results?

Take 10 minutes and write down the learnings. You should be able to find at least 5. If not 50 valuable learning by examining these books.

Stop reading this book for the moment, take 10 minutes and review.

STUDYING THE BOOK MARKET:

LEARNINGS FROM THESE 5 BOOKS:

1. _____
   _____
   _____

2. _____
   _____
   _____

3. _____
   _____
   _____

4. _____
   _____
   _____

---

5. _____

_____

_____

Great. Let's continue.

Now, books are just one way to research your market and gain a greater understanding as to what your target audience responds to.

Let's continue with step 2..

#2) SUMMARIZE 5 MOST SIMILAR COURSE/EVENTS/VIDEOS

Once again, the deeper you research, the greater your understanding of what your audience responds to will be, and the more successful your published book will be.

You may be thinking..

'Bogdan, I am not launching my book yet, I haven't even started writing it, why am I doing this type of research now?'

Great point.

You see, the way you communicate and share your message in your book is arguably as important as your marketing.

Think about what would happen if you did it in reverse *(how most people do it).*

You write your book not fully understanding what your audience wants, needs and responds to.

Then, you do your market research... you gain a deeper understanding... you launch your book with top notch marketing copy (thanks to the research).

Someone buyers your book expecting everything to be communicated in the same way as your marketing copy.

They start reading, super enthusiastic to see more awesomeness.

And... ugh... they are left disappointed because your book messaging is incongruent with your marketing copy.

All because your target market understanding was different at the time of writing compared to the time of marketing.

Now, of course, you are far too incredible to make that mistake.

Come on, have you seen yourself lately?

Your way to awesome!

I just wanted to point out what others *(not you)* would do, and why it wouldn't work.

Ok, flattery aside.

I hope you now have a deeper understanding of why it's important to have a deeper understanding of your audience.

Anyhoo..

It's time for you to research the top 5 courses, events or videos from which you can learn more about your target market.

List the titles in the exercise box:

```
┌─────────────────────────────────────────────────┐
│  5 SIMILAR COURSES/EVENTS/VIDEOS TO LEARN FROM:   │
│    1. _____ │
│    2. _____ │
│    3. _____ │
│    4. _____ │
│    5. _____ │
└─────────────────────────────────────────────────┘
```

Awesome job. Now that you have those new things to research, take 10 minutes and write down what you can learn from these courses, events and videos. The same questions apply.

What benefits are these courses, events, and videos appealing to; what makes people want to buy these courses, events, and videos?

What do these courses, events, and videos do, that you can do with your book, to get similar (and even better!) results?

Now, you don't have to go and attend those events, or go through those courses, just going through the marketing will give you plenty of valuable insight.

Take 10 minutes and list your market research learnings:

```
┌─────────────────────────────────────────────────┐
│              STUDYING THE MARKET:                 │
│                                                   │
│  LEARNINGS FROM THE 5 COURSES, EVENTS & VIDEOS:   │
│                                                   │
│                                                   │
│    1. _____ │
│                                                   │
│       _____ │
│                                                   │
│       _____ │
└─────────────────────────────────────────────────┘
```

2. _____
_____
_____

3. _____
_____
_____

4. _____
_____
_____

5. _____
_____
_____

Brilliant job (if you completed the exercise that is)

Ok, by now, with these 2 exercises, you should have gained a far greater understanding of what exactly what your audience responds to, and how you can use that in your writing and packaging to get great results.

Let's continue..

#3) WRITE LIST OF EVERYTHING YOU KNOW ABOUT THE GIVEN TOPIC

If you're writing a book about gardening, write down EVERYTHING you know about gardening.

If you're writing a book about the socks soldiers wore during World War 2, write a list of EVERYTHING you know about the socks soldiers wore during World War 2.

It doesn't matter what topic you are writing your book about, the key to this step is for you to write a list of EVERYTHING you know about that topic.

Every concept, every strategy, every relevant story, every fact or statistic… write it all down.

'Why?' you may ask..

In stage 3 of the 6 Day Publish Process we will then take everything you know *(this list)* and structure it to form the basis, and framework, for your book.

Plus, it's not productive, or beneficial, for you to be carrying around all of those pieces of wisdom in your mind.

With you constantly making sure you don't forget something very important.

It's not productive during the preparations and pre-work sections.

It's like attempting to fall asleep while your mind is buzzing with thoughts.

This phone number, I need to remember it for tomorrow.

0747 - wait… what was it?

Oh, and these 87 to-do's for tomorrow's to-do list… definitely need to remember those.

Write it down, give you mind a rest.

And at the same time, allow your mind to focus on acquiring even more wisdom for your book as we go along.

So, here's exercise 3 of 4 in this stage of the 6 Day Publish Process.

Right now, take at least 10 minutes and write down a list over absolutely everything you know about your given topic.

However, not just everything you know about the topic... include every relevant story in your list, every relevant example, every metaphor you may include, etc.

Write it all down below.

You ready? Time starts now, go!

YOUR WISDOM LIST ABOUT _____ TOPIC:

- _____
- _____
- _____
- _____
- _____
- _____
- _____
- _____
- _____
- _____
- _____

- _____
- _____
- _____
- _____
- _____
- _____
- _____
- _____
- _____
- _____
- _____

Damn, you're smart!

If you really invested the time and did the exercise, you probably realised that you have more content than you ever thought you did.

Now, don't be limited by me and my template.

If you ran out of space, grab a notepad and keep writing.

This list will become your best friend during stage 3.

And in this context, bigger (and longer) is better!

Keep adding to this list constantly as you learn more about your topic.

Now, let's move onto the last exercise in this stage; *prepare.*

#4) RESEARCH COMPETITION

Just like with the first two exercises, in this exercise, your goal is to find the key competitors *(competitors that are succeeding of course)* that you can learn from, and model.

This includes looking through search results for your topic.

For example, when writing this book, I googled *'how to write a book,'* and read through the topic 10 - 20 articles, forum threads and posts for an even deeper understanding of the market.

This also includes finding the key people, and the key brands, in your market and looking over their marketing copy.

Who are the key people in your industry?

What are the key brands in your industry?

What are the key blogs, forums and platforms in your market that you can look over and review?

Right now, take 5 minutes and research the answers to these questions. Then research what you can learn from those people, those websites, and those brands.

In the words of Anthony Robbins..

'Success leaves clues,'

..meaning that if you want to achieve a certain outcome *(book sales, recognition, etc)* simply find someone who has done it already and model what they are doing.

Don't despise your competition, learn from them.

Stop shipping your own parcels!

This stage *(this chapter)* shouldn't take you more than a few hours (absolute maximum 1 day!) to complete.

You may be thinking..

'Bogdan, you said, read 5 books, that takes more than a few hours.'

In the context of market research, you are not reading those books cover to cover. You are skimming through them (15 - 30 minutes per book) and studying them for market research.

That's why I recommend you buy those 5 similar books on Kindle, and not in paperback format.

This way you can get this whole stage done in a few hours and move on.

Getting your book fully written and published in 6 days or less, that's the goal.

Ok, if you trusted the process, and completed the exercises for this stage, you should now have a much clearer understanding of what your audience want, what appeals to them, and how you can speak to your target audience to get a raving response.

Congratulations on getting here.

To this point... reading these words.

It shows me a lot about your commitment, and I acknowledge you for that. Great job!

Ok, I just got back from Costa.

I'm coffeed up, fed, and ready to share the next stages with you.

It's currently 14:05, 19th of October, 2016.

I'm about 60 pages into this book.

Approaching 10,000 words very soon.

About 1 and a half days into the process.

Now, before we continue…

'WAIT, WAIT, WAIT, Bogdan, what the heck were you doing at Costa, getting coffee. Aren't you supposed to be focused on the book?

Oh, did I forget to mention this.

Immersion is not about trapping yourself in a hotel room. You can leave the hotel room.

What it's about is avoiding distractions.

I just went to a restaurant, ate a meal, and worked for an hour at the restaurant.

Went to Costa, worked for about 10 minutes before my laptop ran out of battery.

It's not about holding yourself hostage in a hotel room for 6 days (well… kinda)

It's about avoiding social media, avoiding distraction, avoiding other work projects, and focusing on just one thing; getting the book published.

Does that make sense?

I'll assume that a yes.

Glad we cleared that up.

Now, let's continue.

In the next section we are going to dive into stage 2 of the 6 Day Publish Process; ***pre-work.***

If there is one stage that most people skip, fail to do properly (and pay the price for) its this stage. Stage 2.

This stage is crucial.

Meanwhile, if you do follow through and go through this stage rigorously, it makes the entire book writing process 10 times easier *(and it gives you much better results in the long term as well!)*

Without further ado, go to the next page, and let's continue with with the very next stage..

SECTION 5:

STAGE 2: PRE-WORK

CHAPTER 8: YOUR PUBLISHING BLUEPRINT

Imagine you're in Tokyo… or in Paris… or Hong Kong.

It's getting late. You're tired. You want to get back to your hotel room.

You're in a city that you don't know.

You don't know the way back.

You get into your rental car… and you just start driving in any direction, hoping to get back to the hotel.

You ignore the road signs.

Navigation, GPS… you ignore those too.

You just drive in random directions.

How likely is it that you will get back to your hotel room quickly and efficiently (if at all)?

Not very likely, huh?

It seems pretty stupid to ignore all directions.

Yet, how often do people start working on a project, or a task, without a clear purpose… without a clear plan?

The answer… more often than you would think.

You see, the clearer you can get on the purpose, and the plan, for your book, the better *(and the more efficiently)* you will get the results you want.

Here's the **PRE-WORK** stage of the 6 Day Publish Process:

PRE-WORK
- MARKET PROBLEM ANALYSIS
- BUYER CUSTOMER AVATAR
- DIFFERENTIATION FACTOR ANALYSIS
- DISRUPTIVE IDEA ANALYSIS
- BUYING HOOK ANALYSIS

- EDUCATIONAL PURPOSE
- COMMERCIAL PURPOSE

- MARKETING & PROFIT STRATEGY ANALYSIS
- PUBLISHING STRATEGY

This stage; *pre-work*, is made up of 3 main parts:

- ANALYSIS
- PURPOSE
- STRATEGY

After you go through this simple, yet powerful, set of exercises you will become infinitely clearer on what, why, and how you can get your book written and published in 6 days, or less.

ANALYSIS:

During this chapter, you will get the chance to go through 5 exercises that will help you analyse your market, your differentiation in that market and the selling points of your book.

During this chapter, you will uncover what's called your DISRUPTIVE IDEA; your one key idea that hooks your audience in, gets them to buy your book, and gets them to read it. This is what will differentiate you from the competition, and will become the centerpiece of all of your marketing, promotion and positioning.

PURPOSE:

During this chapter you will focus on both the educational; and commercial purposes of your book. The clearer you can get on these two things, the easier (and more effective) your book publishing process will be.

STRATEGY:

What is your marketing & profit strategy?

What is your publishing strategy?

If you're not focusing on these things before you start writing your book, you may just be completely wasting your time.

This entire stage (all 9 steps) shouldn't take you any more than a few hours to complete.

Yet, these few hours will set the framework for your entire book, and may just save you many days of work during the rest of this 6 Day Publish Process.

Ok, that's enough preview.

Let's get started with stage 2; *pre-work..*

CHAPTER 9: ANALYSIS

AGONY! PAIN!

Why does this hurt so much?

Are these made out of knife blades?

'I'll do anything to eliminate this pain'

Let's rewind a bit..

I remember my first guitar lesson.

I just got a new guitar, got a coach/teacher, and was ready to learn.

I was SOOOO excited!

I learned the first few basic chords, and started playing them.

My teacher kept telling me..

'If you want it to sound better, push your fingers down on the strings harder.'

And the harder I pushed down, the better the guitar sounded.. however the pain in my fingers increased too.

Of course, this pain goes away fairly quickly as your fingers get used to the strings and chords, however I remember repeatedly thinking to myself..

'I wish I could eliminate this pain, whilst still getting better guitar results'

(Ok, maybe the pain wasn't THAT bad. Frankly, I can't remember… this was a long time ago. I do remember it being pretty damn painful though.)

Here's the lesson:

If someone offered me a product, strategy and/or solution to stop the pain of the guitar strings, I would have bought it in an instant.

People don't buy products, they buy solutions to solve 'pains' in their lives.

Pain; whether it's physical, mental, emotional… whatever pain it is in that person's life… that's why they buy products or services.

People don't buy books.

People buy solutions to the 'pains' in their lives, or opportunities for greater success, happiness and freedom.

Which brings me onto the first exercise in this chapter.

See how that all panned out.

Btw.. see how the chapter starts with a story that hooks your attention, and only then links back to content.

See how it works. *(I'll share more about this later on in this book)*

You see, as a book writer you don't get to simply read books anymore, you get to analyse, examine and study books as you read them.

As you read any book, ask yourself..

Why did he/she (the author) write that?

Why did he/she start that chapter like that?

Why did he/she share that story at that point?

Anyhoo..

#1) MARKET PROBLEM ANALYSIS.

What need, or want, is your book filling in the market?

What gaps are there in the market that you can fill with your book?

Here's an example of what this exercise looks like (this is the MARKET PROBLEM ANALYSIS for this book):

> *The challenge is that most people want to write a book, but they struggle to get it done. They struggle to get it complete... and they struggle to get it marketed and promoted.*
>
> *At the same time, most people think that it takes weeks, months and even years of deep thought and creativity to write a book; they wait for the right moment (which doesn't exist!)*

Most people lack the inspiration, and training, to be able to 'write a book in 6 days' and it limits their business and personal potential.

Lacking credibility? Lacking marketing for your business? Want to discover the greatest tool for marketing your business that will boost your credibility, make you the go-to expert in your industry, and help you market your business.

That tool is your book.

The 'book writing' market has books that share a step-by-step system for getting a book written. The 'book writing' market, however, lacks a book that layouts a system for getting a book written quickly and efficiently (in 6 days, or less.)

To summarize, there is no book that effectively shares how people can turn an idea into a published book in as little as 6 days. This book fills that need.

See how it works?

You are essentially using the market research you have done in stage 2 to identify the gaps in the market that your book can fill.

This research later becomes your differentiation in the market.

And yes, you guessed it, now it's your turn.

It's your turn to complete your **market problem analysis**.

Take at least 10 minutes *(or as long as you need)* to complete the market problem analysis for your book:

MARKET PROBLEM ANALYSIS:

_____

_____

_____

_____

_____

_____

_____

_____

_____

_____

_____

_____

_____

_____

Awesome job.

With each of these exercises you should gain greater and greater clarity about your target market, your book and your book messaging.

#2) BUYER CUSTOMER AVATAR

In the words of Peter Drucker..

'The aim of marketing is to know and understand the customer so well the product or service fits him and sells itself'

Your customer avatar is essentially your ideal customer.

The difference being that you want to name your customer avatar, give him or her a background, a history and a story.

This way, when you are writing, your goal is to talk to this person.

Your goal when writing is to speak directly to the customer avatar you create. This way, your ideal customers will feel like you are talking directly to them during your book.

For example, here is the **buyer customer avatar** for this book:

> *Name: David*
> *Age: 33*
> *Gender: Male*
> *Marital Status: Married*
> *Location: New York, USA*
> *Occupation: Office Employee: Business owner, recently moved to being self-employed.*
> *Annual Income: ...was $100,000/yr ... recently became unpredictable*
> *Education Level: Completed college*
>
> *Background:*
>
> *David, age 33, has been involved in personal development and self help for a number of years now. He has been to dozens of event, has read dozens of books, but hasn't been getting the results he really wants.*
>
> *David wants financial freedom, he want to build a high-6/7 figure business, so he can travel more, never have to worry about money ever again, and so he can live his dreams.*

David dabbled with the thought of starting a business for many years. It all changed last year when David stopped dabbling and committed to making his new business a success. He quit his job to focus on his business full-time. In the last 12 months, David's business has grown at an astounding rate. However, David is ambitious and wants to take it to the next level, fast.

David wants to speak on stages, on media and on platforms, but it's just not happening for him. His friends and family tell him that this is the perfect next step for him and that his message needs to be heard - he know's they are right. He has also dabbled with the idea of writing a book for a while, as he knows that becoming a 'published author' will help him get his message out there, will help him grow this business, and will help him boost his credibility. It's the perfect next step.

The challenge is that David has wanted to write a book for a few months now, yet he hasn't. He doesn't know where to start. He has expertise, however, he doesn't know what to write. He's scared it won't be good enough. He's confused. What can he do?

Now, it's your turn:

BUYER CUSTOMER AVATAR:
_____
_____
_____
_____
_____
_____

As I have said probably about a dozen times already, for no other reasons, other than, that this is critically important, with each of these exercises, you should find yourself with new understanding of your book purpose, your targeting and your ideal messaging.

#3) DIFFERENTIATION FACTOR ANALYSIS

There he was..

..standing there.. roaring.

The tiger approached the roaring lion, and asked:

'Why are you roaring like a fool?'

The lion responded:

'They call me the king because I advertise'

Here's the lesson:

Find things that you can do better than anyone else *(your differentiating factors)* and roar them out loud for the world to hear.

This example is modified version of a brilliant teaching by a direct-response marketing legend by the name of Dan Kennedy.

(Just thought I should to mention that. I don't want credit for something I don't deserve credit for)

Here are just a few of the key differentiating factors for this book:

- A **proven step-by-step system** for turning an idea into a published book. A start to finish, step-by-step, system.

- Become a published author in **6 days, or less.**

- This isn't a book you read. It's a book you DO. A manual **full of exercises and processes that get results.**

Your differentiating factors.. these are your selling points... the benefits for your audience that make your audience want to buy *YOUR* book compared to other books available in your industry.

It's your turn. List the top 2-4 differentiating factors for your book:

```
┌─────────────────────────────────────────────────────────┐
│           DIFFERENTIATION FACTOR ANALYSIS:                │
│                                                           │
│     •    _____       │
│                                                           │
│     •    _____       │
│                                                           │
│     •    _____       │
│                                                           │
│     •    _____       │
│                                                           │
└─────────────────────────────────────────────────────────┘
```

Now, let's go to the next level, and move on to what is called… your DISRUPTIVE IDEA.

#4) DISRUPTIVE IDEA ANALYSIS

I first learned this concept at an event a year of so ago, and it has been of huge impact on my life since.

Your disruptive idea is similar to your differentiating factors, with a slight difference.

It's just **one** idea that becomes the attention grab for your book.

Your disruptive idea is the one sentence that you shout from the rooftops.

Your disruptive idea is something that has the potential to re-shape the focus of an entire industry.

There's no prizes for figuring out what the disruptive idea for this book is… it's front and center..

'Turn an idea into a published book in 6 days, or less'

That one disruptive idea becomes the centerpiece of all of the writing and all of the marketing for this book.

The disruptive idea for my first book, Skilled Success, was…

'Making learning and skill development, harder, more stressful and more time-consuming (Yet far more effective)'

Let's look at some of the other great personal development and success books, and the disruptive ideas that put them on the map:

Here are some examples:

Think & Grow Rich by Napoleon Hill.

The disruptive idea is right there in the title. When this book was first published, this was a disruptive idea in the personal development/self help industry. While every other author was writing about *'take action and work hard to become rich,'* this idea stood out. And in the long term, this disruptive idea changed the focus of the entire self help/personal development industry.

Outliers by Malcolm Gladwell.

The disruptive idea isn't so front and center for this book, however, essentially, the disruptive idea behind this book is that success isn't a matter of intelligence, ambition, genetics, or luck, it's a science, and that there is a scientific formula, *'the 10,000 hour rule,'* to achieving mastery and success.

Let's do one more.

Influence by Dr. Robert Cialdini

At the time of publishing, while other authors, still perceived persuasion as an art, Robert Cialdini, talks about persuasion as a science. A disruptive idea that changed the focus, and the understanding, of an entire industry.

Now, you may be thinking..

*'Wow, if it's that important that I have a great **disruptive idea**, I should probably spend a lot of time focusing on find my disruptive idea.'*

Yes. And no.

Yes, it's important, and put in the work to identify your ***disruptive idea.***

And no, don't over-complicate this.

Your disruptive idea can evolve and change over time.

So, now it's your turn. *What's your **disruptive idea**?*

DISRUPTIVE IDEA ANALYSIS:

My one sentence disruptive idea is...

_____

_____

_____

Awesome. You're on the right track.

#5: BUYING HOOK ANALYSIS

Your buying hook analysis is essentially like an elevator pitch for your book.

If you had 30 seconds, or less, to sell your ideal customer a copy of your book, what would you say?

This will later be refined to become the text for the back cover of your book.

For an example, simply turn to the back cover of this book.

BUYING HOOK ANALYSIS:

_____

_____

_____

_____

_____

_____

_____

_____

_____

_____

_____

_____

_____

_____

Brilliant, in the next chapter we will dig into the purpose of your book.

What is the ultimate outcome you want to help your audience achieve?

What is the educational purpose of your book?

Now, what about the money?

What is the commercial purpose of your book?

Are you simply planning on writing a book and teaching your audience some stuff. The end?

Unless you have the stuff in this next chapter down, you are leaving money on the table and limiting your influence.

Don't worry though, I've got your back.

Let's continue..

CHAPTER 10: PURPOSE

Opened, March 19th, 1932, it stands as one of the centerpieces of Sydney.

With more than 160,000 vehicles driving across everyday, with a surface area of 60 sports fields, it's a sight to behold.

What I'm talking about is the Sydney Harbour Bridge.

Now, just like the Sydney Harbour Bridge, or any other bridge around the world, your book is like a bridge.

Your potential customers are on one side, wanting to get across.

Your bridge, your book, is designed to take people from one side to their desired destination, the other side.

This chapter is made up of two core parts:

- EDUCATIONAL PURPOSE
- COMMERCIAL PURPOSE

..and for the best (and most efficient) book results, you need to have both figured out before you even start writing.

#1) EDUCATIONAL PURPOSE

Imagine attending a live event where the presenter doesn't know what he/she wants to teach you, and where he/she wants to take you (the ideal outcome).

That presenter's presentation would be all over the place.

It wouldn't be very impactful.

Meanwhile, if you DO have a clear educational purpose..

..'I want to take my customers (my readers) from here.. (current results) to over there.. (ideal outcomes)..'

..you will leave a far greater impact on your customers.

Here's an example; here's the ***educational purpose*** for this book:

> *Two main types of people will be reading this book. Either someone who has already published books before (and wants to accelerate the progress for their next books), or someone who has never written a book before (and wants to!)*
>
> *The educational purpose of this book is to take either one of those people, and share, **in a step-by-step, actionable way**, that…*
>
> **1.** *It's possible to get a book written and published in 6 days, or less.*

2. Not just anyone, but THEY can turn an idea into a published book in 6 days, or less, and..

3. To share EVERYTHING, from start to finish, someone must know to get a book written and published in 6 days, or less. Everything from the pre-work, to scheduling 6 days into their calendar, to writing, to getting it published.

The goal: to share, in detail, the entire 6 Day Publish Process, and support readers to implement it.

I want to take the readers to... 1... a place of complete conviction that it's possible... and 2... to a place where they have gotten their book's written and published in a period of 6 days, or less.

That's the educational purpose for this book... and it's crucial that your crystal clear on the educational purpose for your book.

Here are the key questions for you to ask yourself, and then answer:

1. What is the end results you want your book to help the reader achieve?

2. What key pieces of information, stages, do you want to share, and take readers through, to help your readers get to that desired result?

Let's go back to the bridge metaphor for a moment..

Imagine that your ideal customer is standing on one side of a river, and wants to get to the other side of the river.

Your book is the bridge that lets that person get across, however, there are probably a few key steps that your ideal customer needs to take before they can get to the other side.

You need to be clear on those steps and list them in the **educational purpose** of your book.

Anyhoo..

I could have done a better results answering the second question in more detail, but I hope you get the point *(and do a better job than I did!)*

It's your turn.

Stop reading right now and complete this exercise..

EDUCATIONAL PURPOSE:

_____

_____

_____

_____

_____

_____

_____

_____

_____

_____

_____
_____
_____
_____

Great.

That just leaves us part 2 of this chapter..

#2) COMMERCIAL PURPOSE

No matter whether you are a..

..Wall Street loving, materialistic, Lamborghini-wanting, money-obsessed, stock trader..

..a non-materialistic, hippy-loving, nature-loving, spiritual being brought down to earth to spread love and light with people..

..or anything in between.

No matter where you fall on that scale, you need to understand that the best and fastest way to get your message out there, reaching the most amount of people, is if your book has commercial viability.

If spreading the value in your book isn't a self-sustaining system, you are limiting the expansion and reach of your message, because you can't market to reach as many people as you could otherwise.

And I'm gonna tell you something that will seem counter-intuitive (yet is very powerful)..

You ready?

The money is not in the book.

That's right, if you're a business owner planning to write a book to grow your business, you need to understand this more than anyone else.

Yes, your book will make you money.

And yes, it's possible to become rich from your book alone *(a small percentage of people do)*..

..but in the most part, the money is in what comes after your readers buy and read your book.

With that said, most people write books with no commercial purpose.

Most people think that their book is the end of the journey.

Meanwhile, the smart authors, and the smart entrepreneurs realise that their book is simply the beginning of the relationship.. the beginning of the journey that their customers can take with them.

So, I ask you..

What's next?

What does your book lead to?

At the end of your book, what is your call-to-action?

For my first book, *Skilled Success*, the last few pages were dedicated to promoting a bonus video which would bring people into an event that I help lead, teach and facilitate all around the world.

That was the next step for the readers of *Skilled Success*.

So right now, take 5 minutes and write out the commercial purpose for your book.

(If you haven't thought about this before, you may need to spend more time on this… and make sure you DO… this is important!)

COMMERCIAL PURPOSE:

_____

_____

_____

_____

_____

_____

_____

_____

_____

_____

_____

Awesome.

In the next chapter, we are going to go through the final 2 exercises in this stage; *pre-work.*

Remember, the clearer you are on the purpose of your writing, the more effective and impactful your writing will be.

CHAPTER 11: STRATEGY

Before we start, I want to say thank you and congratulations.

Thank you for your attention (and your trust in this process)

And, congratulations.

Congrats on getting to this point.

Did you know that, research by the American Association of Publishers, and USA TODAY, shows that 82% of adults in America want to write a book.

Want to take a guess about what percentage actually DO write a book, or should I just tell you…?

Less than 1%!

Yes, less than 1% of people follow through and get their books written and published.

Those statistics are damn right depressing.

What uplifting is the fact that you are reading these words, following thought and moving closer and closer..

Closer and closer to the day when you can finally hit that *'PUBLISH'* button and become a published author.

Ok, let's continue..

This chapter consists of two main parts *(2 final pre-work exercises)*:

- MARKETING & PROFIT STRATEGY ANALYSIS
- PUBLISHING STRATEGY

Let's begin..

#1) MARKETING & PROFIT STRATEGY ANALYSIS

How are you marketing your book?

Where are you going to get your customers?

What advertising & marketing channels can you test and take advantage of, in order to get prospects and buyers for your book?

How are you pricing your book?

What bonuses can you offer with your book to make it even more valuable?

What other products can you sell alongside your book (audiobooks, checklists, video courses, coaching, etc)?

Now, with this exercise, you don't have to have all the answer figured out right away, however, the more answers you do have figured out right away, the better.

In other words, make sure you refer back to this exercise further on this in the 6 Day Publish Process, come back to it and ensure you complete it.

MARKETING & PROFIT STRATEGY ANALYSIS:

And last, but not least..

#1) PUBLISHING STRATEGY

In this book, we are going to talk about self-publishing, and publishing through CreateSpace, an Amazon company.

Frankly, if you know how to market products through online and offline media..

..self-publishing is the fastest way to get your book in the hands of customers, and start reaping rewards from day 1.

With that said, chances are, later on, this book will also be updated with other publishing strategies including traditional publishing.

Again, you don't need to have this exercise all figured out just yet, but if you do, then that's awesome.

How are you getting your book published?

What publishing channels are you going to deploy?

PUBLISHING STRATEGY:

_____

_____

_____

_____

_____

_____

_____

_____

The more rigorously you completed the pre-work exercises, the easier the rest of the 6 Day Publish Process will be for you.

Remember to refer back to these exercises regularly for the best publishing results.

In the very next section, we are going to dig into stage 3; ***present.***

By the end of this stage, you will not only have a completed book title, subtitle and fully branded book, but you will also have a complete overview for your book.

A complete overview, meaning a ready-to-write template for your book.

Every section.

Every chapter.

Fully mapped out, ready for you to write.

You've done the pre-work, time to get into the book, and start turning your idea into something magical.

Something that will change lives.

Something that will spread, and share, your message with people all around the world; your book.

SECTION 6:

STAGE 3: PRESENT

CHAPTER 12: CRAFTING A KILLER BOOK BRAND

Size doesn't matter.

Looks don't matter.

Don't judge a book by it's cover.

These cliche sayings… we say them, yet we don't actually believe them.

The truth is, looks do matter.

And… don't judge a book by the cover… well, sorry to disappoint, but everybody subconsciously judges a book by it's cover.

Hence, you book cover and your book branding needs to be top notch. It needs to be exceptional.

When it comes to your book making a strong first impression, your book branding is the single most important element of your book, and this should be the part that you deliberate on the most.

Let's do some 80/20 analysis for a moment..

Imagine that you are scrolling through the book section on *Amazon.com*, or some other booksite on the internet you choose, looking for some new, interesting books to read on your favourite book topics..

What 20% of a book makes up about 80% of the buying decision?

- The title
- The subtitle
- The cover design (plus, the colours)
- The author name (plus, author suffix)
- The spine text & design
- The back cover headline
- The back cover text
- The first few pages of the book *(look inside tool)*
- The price

Those 9 things (that 20%) about your book makes up about 80% of the buying decision for your prospects…

..meaning you better nail those 9 things.

Here is the checklist for this chapter:

PRESENT
- BOOK TITLE
- BOOK SUBTITLE/S
- COLOUR PREFERENCES AND ANALYSIS
- AUTHOR + AUTHOR CREDITS

In this chapter, we are going to look at 4 key steps that will help ensure the success of your book:

- CRAFTING A KILLER BOOK TITLE
- CRAFTING A KILLER BOOK SUBTITLE
- COLOUR PREFERENCES & ANALYSIS
- AUTHOR + AUTHOR CREDITS *(AUTHOR SUFFIX)*

Let's dive in with this chapter, and let's create your book brand.

#1) CRAFTING A KILLER BOOK TITLE

Imagine you are standing there..

17 other candidates surrounding you..

And you all know, all 18 of you know, that there can be only 1 victor... there can only be 1 winner..

Have you ever seen, or heard of, any of these TV programmes...

The X Factor, American Idol, Big Brother, The Apprentice, The Voice, America's Got Talent, I'm A Celebrity, Get Me Out Of Here!, Dancing With The Stars..

..have you ever heard of any of those programmes, or any other TV programmes, that start with many potential winning candidates and end with only one winner?

Ok, now I have to ask you an important question..

How do these TV programmes pick a winner?

Pause for a moment and think about it *(this is important)*.

Ok, here's the answer...

..but filtering out all the... let's call them non-winners, shall we?... until they have just one person left

That's how these shows pick the best *(or at least the most popular)* person to become the winner.

And that's the philosophy you should follow for creating a title for your book.

List dozens and dozens of potential candidate titles, then filter titles out until you are left with just one left - the best title.

Now, during this part of the chapter I will share many strategies for finding a great book title, but chances are, you already have ideas buzzing in your mind.

That's just I'm gonna start the exercise here.

I want you to refer back to this few pages *(this exercise)* many, many time *(every time you have a new title idea)*, and write down your new idea in the exercise box below.

Before you start filtering out titles, and before you decide on your final winning title, I want you to give it at least 24 hours.

During those 24 hours, attempt to come up with at least 20 title ideas that you can sort through. Really think about it.

BOOK TITLE IDEAS:

- _____
- _____
- _____
- _____
- _____
- _____

If you run out of space for this exercise, just grab a notepad and continue your list *(the bigger your list starts as, the better)*

Now, let's dig into what makes a killer book title.

Pretty much all successful non-fiction book titles check these 3 boxes when it comes to their title.

1. Attention-Grabbing
2. Memorable
3. Easily communicable

If you are brainstorming book titles and your book title doesn't meet **ALL 3** of these criteria, then simply move on... that's not the right title for your book.

Let break down what each one of these 3 criteria mean:

1. ATTENTION-GRABBING

This is the goal of your title, to grab the attention of your reader, and get them to keep reading... keep reading the subtitle, the back cover, etc.

Nowadays, we are bombarded with brands, titles, names, slogans, and for yours to really stand out, it must be different... and it must be attention-grabbing.

Now, what makes something so-called attention-grabbing really comes down to context.

What can make a title attention-grabbing in the gardening niche is very different from what makes a title attention-grabbing in the space exploration niche.

At the end of the day, the better you understand your market, and more specifically, your ideal customer, the better you will be at picking a great title for your book *(that's why we went through all those pre-work exercises).*

You see, there are many ways to make a title attention-grabbing.

And don't worry, I've got your back, I'll explain these ways in more detail later on in the chapter.

2. MEMORABLE

If you look at the best book titles, and the best books, out there, you will quickly realise that the best book titles are titles you just can't forget… they are titles that get stuck and encoded into your mind.

You must understand though, memorable is not the same thing as attention-grabbing.

Something can be very attention-grabbing, but not memorable.

The best ways to make a title memorable are to make the title…

1… different from everything else out there… and **2**… exceptional *(bigger, better, bolder… and yes, different.)*

And that moves us onto the last title selection requirement..

3. EASILY COMMUNICABLE

If your title matches this selection requirement, you are not guaranteed to have an incredible book title, however, with that said, if your book title doesn't match this selection requirement, it will hugely sabotage the success of your book *(and we don't want that)*

For example *'Easily Communicable'* wouldn't be the best book title, because frankly, it's a nightmare to pronounce.

You want to make your book title easy to say, easy to pronounce and easy to communicate to others.

Want to test if your book title is easily communicable?

Get 10 - 20 people together, and play *Chinese Whispers* with your book title.

This will give you pretty accurate feedback about how easily communicable, or not, your title is.

These 3 selection criteria act like a bouncer… a gatekeeper.. at a club, or a bar.

Their job isn't to just let everybody in, their job is to filter out the people that don't deserve to get in, from those on the list *(and from the VIP's of course)*

Remember, not everybody gets in.

Not everybody gets past the gatekeepers.

The same applies to your book title selection.

If your title idea doesn't very clearly meet all 3 selection criteria *(attention-grabbing, memorable, and easily communicable),* then it doesn't get deserve to go into the club.

Now, let me answer a common question, or two, before we continue..

Question: *Does my book title have to be informative?*

The answer..

Yes, and no.

It does have to be relevant, but it doesn't have to be quote-on-quote, informative.

If you study the titles of the best and most successful books, you will find that most of the titles are not necessary informative. Instead, often, it's the subtitle that shares with readers the information, and the benefits, of reading the book.

Here are some examples of a few successful books:

Who Moved My Cheese?: *An Amazing Way to Deal with Change in Your Work and in Your Life.*

Black Box Thinking: *Marginal Gains and the Secrets of High Performance.*

The Chimp Paradox: *The Acclaimed Mind Management Programme to Help You Achieve Success, Confidence and Happiness.*

Purple Cow: *Transform Your Business by Being Remarkable.*

Those are just a few examples of book titles that aren't necessary informative, and where the subtitle does the informing instead.

On the contrary, yes, an informative book title is great too. Here are some examples of those:

The 7 Habits of Highly Effective People

How to Win Friends and Influence People

Advanced Selling Strategies

Therefore, informative is not one of the core selection criteria, but it's definitely something you should consider.

Ok, let's continue..

Let's jump into the main title patterns of the most successful books, so you can deploy these proven title structures to come up with more incredible titles for your filter-out title idea list.

1. THE BENEFIT TITLE

The first type of title structure you can use is *the benefit title.*

In this proven title structure, you are essentially making a promise, and/or giving a benefit, to your audience.

Here are some examples of benefit titles:

- *The 4-Hour Workweek*

- *How To Win Friends and Influence People*

- *Content That Converts*

- *Think And Grow Rich*

These are all examples of benefit titles. They all share a benefit in the title that can capture the attention of a potential book buyer.

2. THE CURIOSITY TITLE

This is how most books in the non-fiction arena are titled.

Titled in a way where curiosity become the attention hook that gets people to read the subtitle, back cover, and eventually buy.

In order to make this title structure work though, you need a strong, informative subtitle to turn curiosity into actual interest.

Let's use this example:

Purple Cow

That's the title of a book about marketing by Seth Godin.

Now, the name by itself is not informative, it's not benefit-driven, but is sure as heck does grab the attention of people in that market (including me).

It's a great curiosity title.

Also, it's not about randomly picking any words to become your curiosity title, the words *'Purple Cow'* have meaning in the book.

On top of that, if that book, *'Purple Cow,'* had no subtitle, or other text, to share information about the book, that curiosity would very quickly turn to disengagement.

Here's the title together with the subtitle..

Purple Cow: *Transform Your Business by Being Remarkable*

Now it makes more sense. Now, thanks to that subtitle, the curiosity now turns into interest rather than disengagement.

So, right now, you have two tools in your book title creation toolbelt.. *the benefit title* and *the curiosity title.*

You must understand, one tool is not better than the other.

The goal is to give you multiple tools *(a toolbox of tools)* so that you can use the right tool, at the right time, to get the results you want.

Imagine that you had to screw in a screw, but you only had a hammer in your toolbox.

Sure, maybe somehow you would find a way to hammer that screw in, but it would be a heck of a lot more effective to just use the right tool, a screwdriver, to get the job done.

Hence, allow me to give you one more book title creation tool, and a few more book subtitle creation tools, for your toolbox..

Let's continue..

3. THE SHOCK TITLE

These titles can sometimes feel like a slap to the face for your target audience, however they can work very well *(if executed correctly)*

Here are some examples:

Networking Is Not Working (this is the book title)

..which is followed by a *benefit subtitle*..

Stop Collecting Business Cards and Start Making Meaningful Connections (this is the book subtitle)

Or these examples:

Trust Me, I'm Lying: *Confessions of a Media Manipulator*

..or lastly, this one..

How To Be F*cking Awesome: *Sticking A Finger Up To The Law Of Attraction And A Thump Up To Action*

Now, you must know, these titles are polarizing. No doubt about it.

Meaning, they will bother and disqualify a percentage of people *(which is a good thing btw..)*

Here's what Tim Ferriss said about polarizing your audience:

The 4-Hour Workweek also bothered some people and was ridiculed by others, which I took as a positive indicator. It's not accidental that Jay Leno parodied the book on-air — the title lends itself to it, and that was by design. You can't have strong positive responses without strong negative responses, and beware — above all — the lukewarm reception from all. 'Oh, that's nice. I think it's pretty good,' is a death sentence.

Audience polarization is a good thing.

In fact, it's a great thing.

You can't make everyone like you... and the only way to make people love you *(become raving fan customers)* is to express sides of yourself *(beliefs, stories, opinions)* that other people will hate, and be repelled by.

If you don't have haters, you won't have die-hard fans of you, and your work, either.

The choice is yours..

Anyhoo..

..there you go, you now have 3 book title creation tools that you can pull out at any moment, and use to get the results you're after.

Now, as you have probably realised already, your subtitle, in most cases, is an important part of your book brand.

So, how exactly can you craft a killer book subtitle?

That's the question we are going to answer next.

#2) CRAFTING A KILLER BOOK SUBTITLE

Once again, most successful book subtitles fall under only a few core subtitle structures.

Now, the goal is to knock this entire subtitle question out of the park in one shot, that's why are going to start with the one subtitle structure that most successful books use, either consciously or unconsciously, to get incredible results..

1. THE DISRUPTIVE IDEA SUBTITLE

And the best part is that, if you have done the exercises in stage 2 of this 6 Day Publish Process, you may just have your subtitle already figured out for you.

In this subtitle structure, your disruptive idea actually becomes your subtitle.

For example, this book..

..the disruptive idea of this book is..

Turn your idea into a published book in 6 days, or less

And yes, you know it, that also became the subtitle for this book.

That's because that one sentence, above all else, sells this book incredibly well.

So, what is your disruptive idea?

That's your first subtitle idea.

Now, just like with the book title, the best way for you to identify and pick the best subtitle for your book is in TV programme disqualification style.

And yes, you guessed it, it's time for you to make your subtitle list.. *(list as many subtitle as you can, then start filtering out until you have a winner)*

BOOK SUBTITLE IDEAS:

- _____
- _____
- _____
- _____
- _____
- _____
- _____
- _____
- _____
- _____
- _____
- _____
- _____
- _____

- _____
- _____
- _____
- _____
- _____
- _____
- _____
- _____
- _____
- _____
- _____
- _____
- _____
- _____
- _____
- _____
- _____
- _____
- _____
- _____

And once again, I don't want to give you just one tool.

That would make a pretty lame subtitle creation toolbox if it has just one tool in it.

That's why I am going to give you 2 more subtitle creation tools. This way you can always have the right tool to get the job done.

2. THE CLARIFYING SUBTITLE

This tool, *the clarifying subtitle*, is especially handy when you have opted to go for a curiosity title.

Here are some examples:

Pre-Suasion: *A Revolutionary Way to Influence and Persuade*

The One Thing: *The Surprisingly Simple Truth Behind Extraordinary Results*

Weapons of Math Destruction: *How Big Data Increases Inequality and Threatens Democracy*

The subtitle takes the title and clarifies it for greater understanding; that's a *clarifying subtitle.*

And lastly, here is the 3rd subtitle creation tool for your toolbox..

3. THE AMPLIFYING SUBTITLE

This works bests with a *benefit title.*

Let me give you an example.. then I'll break it down for you..

The 4-Hour Work Week: *Escape the 9-5, Live Anywhere and Join the New Rich*

In this example, the subtitle, amplifies the message of the title.

The 4-Hour Work Week - that title already conveys a benefit for people to buy, and read, the book.

The subtitle of this book *AMPLIFIES* the power of that title.

That's what *the amplifying subtitle* does.

And voila..

..you now have 3 powerful subtitle creation tools in your toolbox.

Now, before you finalise your title, and your subtitle, you need to understand that the most effective way to pick the best title is through testing.

Ask your audience.

Survey your customers.. your friends.. your family.

You don't want to survey them with 50 different titles though, narrow it down to your top 2 or 3, then, if you choose to, start the surveying process to identify the best version of your title.

Don't worry, you don't have to stay on this stage until you find your title, you can continue progressing through the 6 Day Publish Process and come back to finalise your title, and your subtitle, later.

When you do decide on your title, and your subtitle, write it in here to complete this exercise:

YOUR BOOK TITLE AND SUBTITLE:

YOUR BOOK TITLE: _____

_____

YOUR BOOK SUBTITLE: _____

_____

Awesome job.

With each step.. with each page.. and with each exercise, you are moving closer and closer to that moment when you will finally hold that first printed copy of your brand new book..

A big smile on your face.

You did it.

You made it happen!

You are now part of the elite 1% that actually follow through and turn their book ambitions into reality!

Let's keep going, shall we?

#3) COLOUR PREFERENCES AND ANALYSIS

The next step, and in most cases, it's a rather simple one, is to decide what your book brand colours will be.

What colour do you want your title to be in on your book cover?

What colour do you want your book cover background to be?

What colours do you want people to resonate with your book (and your brand)?

Now, before you opt to just choose your favourite colours and move on, you must know that all colours have a meaning.

And whether you like it or not..

..people will judge your book, consciously or subconsciously by the colours *(and by the design)* you choose to use.

For more about what each colour means and portrays to your audience, what colours you should use, and how to choose the perfect colours for your book brand, go to the free bonuses page for this book:

FreeBonuses.6DayPublish.com

Anyway, right now, take 3 - 5 minutes, decide on, and write down, the colours you are going to use for your book.

COLOUR PREFERENCE & ANALYSIS:

_____

_____

_____

_____

_____

And now, the last part of this chapter..

#4) AUTHOR + AUTHOR CREDITS

This is probably the easiest, and shortest part, of this book.

These 2 questions..

1. *What name are you going to have on your book cover?*

If your name is Michael Smith, are you going to use the name *'Michael Smith'* on your cover?..

..or *Mike Smith..?*

..or, congratulations for the hard work, *Dr. Michael Smith..?*

And now the second question..

2. *Are you going to use a author suffix line on your cover? And, if yes, what will it be?*

A author suffix line *(or what I call, 'author credits')* is a line after your name that says something like:

'Author of XYZ & CEO of XYZ Inc'

Ok, so are you ready to complete what's probably the simplest, and easiest, exercise in this book?

Of course you are. Here it is:

AUTHOR + AUTHOR CREDITS:

AUTHOR NAME ON COVER: _____

_____

AUTHOR CREDITS *(OPTIONAL):* _____

_____

Brilliant. In the next chapter, we are going to talk about your book overview.

If you complete this next chapter, your book writing process will be about 10X easier. No doubt about it.

The book overview you are about to create will become the framework for your entire book. In other words, it's very important.

Go to the next page, and let's continue..

CHAPTER 13: YOUR WRITING GAME PLAN

It can happen..

It really can.

Look at sports.

Many, many times teams have had star-studded team sheets, yet they haven't won games, won trophies or won championships.

Why is that?

It's because having the right players isn't enough.

You also need the right coaches, who create *the right game plans* for the team to get results.

This applies directly to your book writing and book publishing efforts.

Have you got a game plan?

Yes, you can have what seems like all of the right pieces, you can have all of the right content, the right tips, tricks and the right life-changing strategies, but do you also have a game plan that helps you effectively deploy that content for maximum audience impact.

You need a game plan.

So, what do I mean by a game plan?

And, how can you create one to make your writing 10X easier (and more effective?)

That's what we are going to talk about in this chapter.

I'm super excited about this; this is where we really start getting into the nitty-gritty work that makes your book, not only sell copies, but also change lives.

If only you could see the smile on my face right now as I say those words

(it's smiling big and wide if you haven't figured already...)

Anyhoo, here's the checklist for this chapter:

- SECTION OVERVIEW (Usually 3-9)
- SECTION CHAPTER OVERVIEW (Usually 10 - 30)
- CHAPTER KEY POINT OVERVIEW (Usually 3-8/chapter)
- SECTION BRANDING
- CHAPTER BRANDING

By the end of this chapter, you will have a fully mapped out game plan for each part, for each chapter, and for each section of your incredible book.

Firstly, before I go into explaining what the heck your *section overview (your game plan)* is… what your *section chapter overview* is… and what your *chapter key point overview* is..

..let me just show you.

What you are about to read is the book overview *(the combination of those 3 things; section overview, section chapter overview and chapter key point overview)* for my first book, *Skilled Success.*

I want you to read through this entire book overview it will teach you a huge amount about book structure and book creation.

Trust the process, remember? Ok, you ready?

SKILLED SUCCESS BOOK OVERVIEW:

PREFACE: *WHY THIS BOOK WILL TEACH YOU EXACTLY NOTHING (UNLESS YOU DO THIS)* **[PREFACE]**
- ○ *Attention Grabs (Disruptive Idea)*
- ○ *Align Values*
- ○ *Reduce Skepticism*
- ○ *Align Values & Vision*
- ○ *The One Thing..*
- ○ *Why you can do it..*
- ○ *Benefits of living an accelerated learning life..*
- ○ *It's not your fault!*
- ○ *Story (Reluctant Hero)*
- ○ *Displaying credibility (Earn The Right)*
- ○ *Hook to next chapter*

YOUR ULTIMATE POWER *[SECTION #1]*
- • The lifelong, no-matter-what-happens prosperity secret *[CHAPTER #1]*
  - ○ *Imagine if everything was taken away from you? What would you have left? YOUR SKILL SET.*

- o *Why your skills are your ultimate power...*
- o *Sales/Management/Marketing skill example (World will always need sales people)*
- o *Hook to next chapter*
- *The Lesson Source [CHAPTER #2]*
  - o *My story..*
  - o *Successful people are constant learners*
  - o *Quote.. '$30 out for every $1 to you invest into your own education' (and explain)*
  - o *Your learning plan… life systems*
  - o *Hook to next chapter*
- Power Skills *[CHAPTER #3]*
  - o *Power skills*
    - *Build up importance of power skills*
    - *Examples of power skills*
  - o *Develop Transferable Skills*
  - o *Who makes the most money in jobs? Risk + Skill + Time Commitment*
  - o *Education should teach 3 things*
    - *life/survival skills*
    - *success skills*
    - *mastery skills*
  - o *Hook to next chapter*
- Maximum Value *[CHAPTER #4]*
  - o *Written this way on purpose*
  - o *One key skill to focus on during book*
  - o *Other keys for maximum value...*
    - *Re-read chapters*
    - *3 top ideas: look for 3 top ideas from each chapter and keep asking 'How can I use this to improve my life results?*
    - *Interact with the book and review what your learning..*
    - *Follow the action steps at the end of each section*
  - o *Hook into next section...*

- *Section 1 Implementation*
  - *Introduction to implementation & checklist*
  - *1-2 Implementation Steps for Key Concept 1*
  - *1-2 Implementation Steps for Key Concept 2*
  - *1-2 Implementation Steps for Key Concept 3*

STRATEGIES PROVEN NOT TO WORK *[SECTION #2]*
- A broken system explained *[CHAPTER #5]*
- *Knowledge vs Targeted Knowledge [CHAPTER #6]*
  - *School promotes mediocrity - Learn 85 different skills*
  - *If you look at successful people, they are usually masters at just few skills (that's their focus)*
  - *Would you rather be a master at 1 or mediocre at 80?*
  - *Why are most people broke, miserable and feel lack of freedom and control in their life? The foundations: education*
  - *The education system trains people to be workers, not entrepreneurs*
- *Section 2 Implementation*
  - *1-2 Implementation Steps for Key Concept 1*
  - *1-2 Implementation Steps for Key Concept 2*
  - *2-4 Implementation Steps for Key Concept 3*
  - *Hook into next section...*

THE NEW APPROACH *[SECTION #3]*
- *Action-based learning [CHAPTER #7]*
  - *How do you learn to ride a bike… by reading text books? By going to lectures? Course not, by doing it. Action-based learning*
- The failure myth *[CHAPTER #8]*
  - *Celebrate your failures (They move you towards your success) - Sara Blakely*
  - *Michael Jordan story*
    - *Quote - video*

- *The foundations of action-based-learning [CHAPTER #9]*
  - *Passion: Ignited Passion*
  - *Discipline: Disciplined Training*
  - *Innovation: Constant Innovation To Reach New Levels of Excellence*
- *Teachability Index [CHAPTER #10]*
- *The Learning Process [CHAPTER #11]*
  - *Learn (Cognitive)*
  - *Cognitive Repetition & Integration*
  - *Action (Do)*
  - *Tracking*
  - *Feedback*
  - *Review*
  - *Future Improvements*
- *Section 3 Implementation*
  - *1-2 Implementation Steps for Key Concept 1*
  - *1-3 Implementation Steps for Key Concept 2*
  - *2-4 Implementation Steps for Key Concept 3*
  - *Hook into next section...*

DEVELOPMENT STRATEGIES OF HIGH-ACHIEVERS [SECTION #4]

- *Filtering for lessons vs. being taught*
- *Mentors (Coaching)*
- *Sub-skills - The 80/20 Rule For Training*
  - *Within each skill there are sub-skills, and just like everything else, 20% of sub-skills get you 80% of the results*
- *Memory Triggers*
- *Emotional Learning*
- *Increased difficulty training, making execution easier*
- *Systematized learning & Immersion*
- *Section 4 Implementation*
  - *1-2 Implementation Steps for Key Concept 1*
  - *1-2 Implementation Steps for Key Concept 2*
  - *1-2 Implementation Steps for Key Concept 3*

- 1-2 Implementation Steps for Key Concept 3
- 1-2 Implementation Steps for Key Concept 3
- Hook into next section...

THE ULTIMATE DEVELOPMENT EXPERIENCE *[SECTION #5]*
- *The Next Level*
- *The Next Steps*
  - *Free Bonus Video CTA*

That right there was the 3-4 page game plan *(book overview)* that allowed me to write my first book, *Skilled Success*, a 204 page book, effectively, in 6 days.

Now, you must know, that entire book overview was written before I even wrote the first word of that book.

And yes, I changed bits and pieces of it as I went along and started writing.

And yes, there are things on that book overview that I skipped, and there are also bits that aren't on that book overview *(things I created, and added, as I went along)*

That's the whole point.

This book overview, your writing game plan, is designed to give you a framework that is rigid enough to keep you focused, yet flexible enough to allow your creative spirit to flourish.

If there's one quote that puts this best, and I love this quote, it's this one:

'Give me boundaries, so I can be free'

Let me give you these examples..

If I told you that you are expected to create an incredible theatrical production for 50 select people that you have to put on in 3 weeks time..

..you would probably struggle *(I know I would..)*

We would probably struggle to create something quote-on-quote incredible, because it's too vague of an expectation.

What type of theatrical production?

What theme? How long?

What's the budget?

Who are the 50 selection people?

Kids? Teenagers? Adults? Men? Woment?

In other words, there are no boundaries for your creativity.

Meanwhile, if you were expected to put on a 2 hour jungle-story themed theatrical production, that shares the moral that *'teamwork is important'* to a group of 50 select 8 - 12 year old kids that love to laugh and be entertained. And, you have 3 weeks to put this together with a budget of $100,000 for the production.

Now, you can starting to get a clearer understanding of the expectations, and now within those boundaries, your creativity can flourish.

That's what your book overview is all about.

Ok, so before I get into the specifics, and give you the exercise of creating your very own *book overview*, there are a few things you need to know about section, chapter and book structure.

Books have sections.

Sections have chapters.

Chapters share a few key points specific to that chapter.

A book typically has a preface/intro, 4 - 10 sections, with each section typically containing 2 - 6 chapters, and with each chapter typically sharing 1 - 5 key points *(key ideas)*.

Now, you may be thinking..

'Hey, Bogdan, but there are some books that don't follow all of those rules'

To which my response is..

Exactly. That's the point.

That may be true, however, I can pretty much guarantee that those authors KNOW those rules... know the rules of the game... so that they can break certain ones to get great results.

I was recently studying storytelling; the art of telling stories in an engaging and captivating way.

And I was going through a great storytelling program by a brilliant guy by the name of *Michael Hauge*.

Michael works with top Hollywood movie producers to optimise and refine their screenplays for the best movie results.

He has worked with top people, top movie producers, top screenwriters, and, oh yeah, Will Smith.

That is a pretty awesome credential to have btw... *'i have worked with Will Smith on a movie'*... isn't it?

Anyway, that's not the point.

As I was going through the program I remember Michael saying that he often gets asked the same question over and over..

'But this movie... or this tv show... doesn't follow the storytelling structure you set out... what the deal with that?'

He then went on to start talking about how the best Hollywood producers know all of the rules... know the best practices... and it's only because they know them, and have mastered these rules... that they can then go on to break them to get even better results.

And just like Michael has researched the rules of movie production and storytelling, I have research the rules... the best practices... for book writing, and book creation.

Now, don't get me know... that wasn't a comparison.

Michael has over 20 years of experience in screenwriting and movie production... I haven't even been alive for that long.

With that said though, I don't know many people, *ON THE PLANET* that can achieve the results that I achieve, in the timeframe I achieve them in. Not many people on this planet can get projects completed, like writing a high quality book and getting it published, in the speed I do it in.

And more importantly, not many people on the planet can consciously break down that entire book writing process into a system... a framework... that gets results, consistently.

You can do the research.

Anyhoo..

Michael teaching about knowing the rules of the game..

..and this 100% applies to book creation.

As Einstein put so eloquently:

You have to learn the rules of the game. And then you have to play better than anyone else.

And we can't argue with Einstein...

Writing a chapter.. writing a section.. writing a book.. it's an art and a science.

Especially with a non-fiction book.

Writing a nonfiction book is all about the balance between engagement and content.

Get this balance wrong... and people will finish your book, either bored out of their mind, or feeling no better off than when they started.

You may think..

A nonfiction book... it's all about packing as much content, as many strategies, as much good stuff, in there are possible, huh?

Well, not exactly.

Imagine if I gave you a book about accounting... let's call this book..

..Accounting 101.

(that book title sounds boring enough for this example)

Ok, let's say I hand you a copy of my brand new book, *Accounting 101*, and the entire book is all content.

100% mind-dubbing detail about accounting.

No stories.

Just numbers, data and content.

(now, for the accountants reading this, you must know I love maths… I can do accounting all damn day… I freakin' love it… but many don't feel the same way about accounting.)

Now, you may be thinking..

'Well, surely my audience is smarter than that, they understand that my book is about sharing as much content as possible, huh?'

Maybe you have found that audience *(unlikely, but let's say you have..)*

Firstly, email me at bogdan@bogdanjuncewicz.com, that audience sounds amazing.

I want to get in on that.

Secondly, even if that's what people think they want, odds are they want entertainment and engagement as well.

You want to engage, and entertain your audience while you educate them.

People learn far more effectively, and remember more, when they are actually engaged.

With that said, at the same time, you don't want to over-do it and provide **only** entertainment in your nonfiction book..

..you don't want your audience finishing your book, engaged, inspired, but feeling no better off *(haven't learned anything)*.

It's a balance.

I wish that, as someone who loves instructions and processes, I could tell you..

'Yes, you need exactly 58% entertainment, and 42% content, in your book'..

..but I can't.

It differs depending on thousands of different elements.

What can I tell you is that people rather be entertained, and learn nothing, then learn lot of stuff, but be completely bored out of their mind.

As counter-intuitive as that seems, yes, people have studied this, and found that even if someone is coming specifically to learn something *(a book, a seminar, a conference, etc)* they still rather be entertained than be educated.

Hence, the magic formula is..

..well, there is no magic formula, it's all about balance.

Balance & testing.

Now that you know this, you're way ahead of the thousands of authors and speakers that believe in the myth of *'the more content, the better..'*

Also, now that you know it's all about balance, how do you strike that balance?

What can you do in each chapter, in each section, to both, engage, and educate, your audience?

What you are about to discover is a structural template for a chapter.

First, let me give you an example..

What you are about to read is the very beginning of chapter 7.

However, I don't want you to just read it, I want to study it..

Is this sentence crafted for engagement, or is it crafted for content-delivery?

When does it transition from one to the other?

Think about those questions as you slowly re-read these words.

You ready?

CHAPTER 7: KNOW THY MARKET

Have you ever been at a party, at a meeting, or just hanging out with some friends, when someone calls a cab.. then they ask you..

'Where are you heading?'

You tell them where you are heading.

They say, 'Hey, I'm heading in that direction too, want to share a cab/taxi?'

You say, 'Well, as long as you're already going that way..'

Now, as long as this person isn't an axe murder, this makes perfect sense.

Why take two cabs instead of one, right?

This concept may seem simple, but it's really powerful

Allow me to explain..

You probably don't deliver your own parcels.

You either use the postal service, FedEx, UPS or some other major delivery service, right?

In fact, every merchant who ships products does the same thing.

Pretty much nobody delivers their own packages.

Because FedEx, USPS, and UPS are already going that way.

Those delivery services have the infrastructure in place.

They have planes that are already flying that way. Drivers who are already driving that way.

The incremental cost of adding YOUR package to their route is almost ZERO.

That's because they're already going that way.

But to deliver that package yourself would cost you hundreds of dollars (renting a delivery vehicle, hiring a driver, plane tickets, the cost of your time, etc.)

It would be crazy for you to fly to a certain country just to deliver a package.

And this applies to almost everything: you don't make your own clothes, you don't build your own house, you don't grow your own food...because someone else already has a system in place that is far more efficient.

Now you may be thinking..

'Cool story Bogdan, but what does this have to do with your writing & publishing a book?'

Well... a lot actually.

A lot of people that attempt to write and publish their book attempt to create it from the ground up. From scratch.

They attempt to figure out, on their own, what their audience will want.

They attempt to figure out, on their own, what titles, what contents, what design, what everything, will give them the best publishing results.

They attempt to figure everything out on their own.

Trial and error.

Attempting to create something (a book) from the ground up.

It makes no sense.

Alternatively, imagine if you could discover exactly what your market wants, needs and buys, before you even write a word of your book..

That's what this first part of The 6 Day Publish Process is all about; **preparation***.*

Did you catch the transition?

See how the short story... the parable... became a metaphor for a valuable lesson in the chapter?

See how it works?

See how the chapter doesn't start by sharing content... see how it starts by hooking you into a story... and only then, transitions to the content?

Pretty cool, don't you think?

Yes, there are probably things that can be improved in that story, and in that chapter *(there always are things to improve, in everything!)*, but you get the point.

Every part.. every chapter.. every section is a dance between engagement and content-delivery.

Back and forth they go.

So, here's the structural step-by-step template for a chapter:

1. Engaging, gripping, story intro (ENGAGEMENT)
2. The transition; switching from engagement to content

3. Content delivery; share the lessons (CONTENT)
4. Future pacing (ENGAGEMENT)
5. Hook into next chapter/section

So, you may have a few questions..

1. *Future pacing, Bogdan, what do you mean?*

Future pacing; here's an example:

> *Awesome job.*
>
> *With each step, with each page, with each exercise, you are moving closer and closer to that day when you finally hold that first printed copy of your brand new book.*
>
> *A big smile on your face.*
>
> *You did it.*
>
> *You made it happen!*
>
> *You are now part of the elite 1% that actually follow through and turn their book ambitions into reality!*
>
> *Let's keep going, shall we?*

Future pacing is where you transition your focus back from content delivery to engagement.

In most cases, you want to start, and end, your chapters with the focus on engagement, with content squeezed perfectly in the middle.

Imagine a burger..

(It's kinda strange I'm using a burger metaphor, since I'm a vegan. Oh well… let's roll with it..)

Imagine a burger..

You wouldn't just put some meat on a plate and call that a burger… of course not…

You want to have the meat *(and everything else in the burger)* nicely squeezed between 2 buns.

(FYI… you can completely ignore that example if you choose, as I have little-to-no expertise in the art of burger creation)

The meat *(and all the other stuff that goes on the inside)*… that represents your content.

And, for maximum impact, you want all that content neatly squeezed between 2 buns.

To summarize, in most cases, you want to start and finish your book chapters, and your book sections, with engagement focused writing.

(See what I did there.. added a metaphor… the burger metaphor… to add engagement, in order to teach a lesson? Come on, you wouldn't really expect me to teach something, and not actually implement it?)

I'm getting off track.

Back to future pacing.

Future pacing is a way to turn content-delivery into engagement-delivery.

And at the same time, it's a way to acknowledge your audience, increase the read-through rate of your book, and boost implementation.

Anyhoo, back to the structural step-by-step template.

1. Engaging, gripping, story intro (ENGAGEMENT)
2. The transition; switching from engagement to content
3. Content delivery; share the lessons (CONTENT)
4. Future pacing (ENGAGEMENT)
5. Hook into next chapter/section

And onto question number 2...

> 2. 'Hook into next chapter/section? What's that, why should I do that, and how do I do that?'

The more of your book your audience reads, the more value they should get, the more relationship, and trust, you develop with them, and the better for everyone.

'Hooking into the next chapter/section' is a simple and easy way to boost your book read-through rate *(what percentage of people actually read through and finish your book)*

And no, just because someone bought your book doesn't mean they will read it.

In fact, some studies show that less than 10% of books that get bought ever get read!

It's shocking! *(Yet true)*

That's why, if your book has great value to share within it, it's your obligation to do everything in your power to get that book read.

Here's an example of how, at the end of a chapter/section, you can hook into the next one:

> *Now, let's continue.*
>
> *In the next section, we are going to dive into stage 2 of the 6 Day Publish Process;* **pre-work.**
>
> *If there is one stage that most people skip, fail to do properly (and pay the price for later,) it's this stage. Stage 2.*
>
> *This stage is crucial.*
>
> *If you do follow through and go through this stage rigorously though, it will make your entire book writing process 10 times easier (and it will give you much better results in the long term as well!)*
>
> *Without further ado, go to the next page, and let's continue with stage 2.*

Essentially, your pre-selling the next chapter, or the next section, in the current chapter, or section.

It's like a TV show..

Have you ever seen a TV show and at the end of each episode, or each season, they would leave a cliffhanger, something hooking you into the next episode?

It's exactly like that.

So, there you have it... a basic 5 point step-by-step template for write an engaging and well-structured chapter, or section, for your book.

Plug in your content, your stories, your parables and deploy the template.

And, as I said before, the book rules I am sharing in this book are designed, and crafted, to be broken.

You write a chapter using that structural template.

It rocks. Great job.

In the next chapter, maybe you change it up a bit, maybe you take out the future pacing, and you add another story in there.

That's great to.

Break all the book writing rules laid out in this book if you choose to, just make sure that before you do... *1... you deeply understand the rules laid out in this book...* and *2... you only break these rules with a specific, and proven purpose, that will give you a specific result.*

You don't want to break these rules just because you feel like it, you want to break them to achieve a certain, and specific, outcome *(if you choose that is...)*

Ok, now that we got that all figured out, it's time to go back to the *6 Day Publish* Checklist, and continue your progress from idea to a published book in 6 days, or less.

#1) SECTION OVERVIEW

The first thing you want to do is take everything you know, and want to share, about your topic, and categorize it into 4 - 10 logical sections.

Here's how this book *(the one you are reading right now)* is categorized into 9 different sections:

1. The Thousand Year Old Marketing Tool
2. Are These Myths Holding You Back? (Do This Instead)
3. The 6 Day Publish Process
4. Stage 1: Prepare
5. Stage 2: Pre-work
6. Stage 3: Present **[YOU ARE HERE]**
7. Stage 4: Produce
8. Stage 5: Publish
9. The Next Steps

If I was to write a book about football/ooooor, it might look like this (I don't intend to. That niche is all yours if you choose it.)

1. Benefits Of Living A Footballers Lifestyle
2. This Is What It Takes
3. Finding Your Strengths
4. Committing To A Position
5. Best Training Practices
6. Getting Scouted
7. Going PRO!

See how it logically progresses from section 1 to section 7?

In most cases, the objective for your book will be to take the readers from **A** (current situation) to **B** (desired situation)..

..your *section overview* essentially become a list of the key things your audience needs to know to get from A to B.

Now, before you start creating your *section overview*, let me take you through the next two steps in the checklist.

#2) SECTION CHAPTER OVERVIEW

In this step, you dig deeper and get more specific about what it will take to get your readers from A to B.

What you're doing in this step is breaking down each section into about 2 - 6 different chapters.

Let's take section 5 of this book as an example:

SECTION 5: STAGE 2: PRE-WORK **[This is the section]**

- Your Publishing Blueprint *(overview of the section)*
- Analysis
- Purpose
- Strategy

Those 4 chapters right there are the chapters that make up that section… section 5.

Those 3 chapters: **Analysis, Purpose,** and **Strategy** then breakdown into 8 different parts *(the 8 steps in the **pre-work** stage of the 6 Day Publish Checklist)*

See how it all works?

With each of these 3, (*section overview*, *section chapter overview*, and *chapter key point overview*) you go deeper and deeper. And with each of them you gain greater and greater clarity regarding the contents of your book.

Which brings us onto the the next step...

#3) CHAPTER KEY POINT OVERVIEW

This is the next, and last, step in the ***book overview***.

In this step, you are breaking down each chapter into the 1 - 5 key points you want to convey.

Here's an example:

CHAPTER 13: YOUR WRITING GAME PLAN

- Important Of A Game Plan
    - Star-studded sports team metaphor
    - Importance of having a game plan
- Book Overview
    - Example of *Skilled Success* book overview
    - *'Give me boundaries so I can be free'* quote (balance between rigid and flexible)
    - Putting on a theatrical production - Example
    - Know the rules, so you can break them
        - Michael Hauge storytelling course story
        - Einstein quote
    - The engagement and content-delivery balance
    - Accounting book example
    - 5 step basic structural template
    - How to hook into the next chapter
- Section Overview
    - Example of 6 Day Publish section overview
- Section Chapter Overview
    - Share Example
- Chapter Key Point Overview
    - Example **[YOU ARE HERE RIGHT NOW]**
    - Exercise *(creating your book overview)*
- Section Branding
- Chapter Branding

You can go as deep as you choose.

The black bullet points on the left side... those are the key points.

Now, the write dots, those are one level deeper.

And the black boxes, those are two levels deeper.

It's your book. It's your overview. You can choose how deep you want to go with your game plan.

Just make sure you don't spend 6 days on your game plan *(your book overview)* and you never actually start writing your book.

Don't over-complicate it.

However, do put in the work.

It's also about balance.

Also, I want to apologise for the spoilers with that last example… I really hope you can forgive me.

Now that I spoiled it for you, I guess it's no longer a surprise that now it's your turn to create your *book overview*.

On the next page you'll find a template for you to create your *book overview*.

1. Where you see all of the black dots *(most left)*, add your book sections
2. Where you see all of the white/grey dots, add your chapters
3. Where you see all of the black boxes, add your key points for each chapter.

You do not need to have all of the section and chapter titles figured out yet... that's still to come.

FYI… the more pages this book has, the more I pay, per copy, to get this book in the hands of my customers.

However, I much rather pay more, and include these exercises in the book, so that you can actually follow through and lay the foundations for your publishing success, rather than reduce costs, and not give you the best workbook for publishing success that I possibly can!

BOOK OVERVIEW:

- **(Example overview)** <u>KEY MYTHS PEOPLE BUY INTO!</u>
  - <u>The Slow & Steady Myth</u>
    - <u>Tortoise & hare story</u>
    - <u>Immersion concept</u>
    - <u>4 day publish experiment</u>
  - <u>The Perfection Myth</u>
    - <u>Write. Edit. Write. Edit. Myth.</u>
    - <u>Lean startup book concepts</u>
    - <u>Constant improvement</u>
  - <u>The Jump Straight Into It Myth</u>
    - <u>The importance of planning</u>
    - <u>Don't overplan</u>
    - <u>Balance</u>
  - <u>[BLANK - this section only has 3 chapters]</u>
    - <u>[BLANK]</u>
    - <u>[BLANK]</u>
    - <u>[BLANK]</u>

That was the example.

On the next page is space for you to get started and create your book overview. Turn the page and begin.

YOUR BOOK OVERVIEW:

- [SECTION #1] _____

  - o _____
    - ■ _____
    - ■ _____
    - ■ _____
  - o _____
    - ■ _____
    - ■ _____
    - ■ _____
  - o _____
    - ■ _____
    - ■ _____
    - ■ _____
  - o _____
    - ■ _____
    - ■ _____
    - ■ _____

- [SECTION #2] _____

  - o _____
    - ■ _____
    - ■ _____
    - ■ _____
  - o _____

149

- ■ _____
- ■ _____
- ■ _____
  - ○ _____
    - ■ _____
    - ■ _____
    - ■ _____
  - ○ _____
    - ■ _____
    - ■ _____
    - ■ _____

- **[SECTION #3]** _____
  - ○ _____
    - ■ _____
    - ■ _____
    - ■ _____
  - ○ _____
    - ■ _____
    - ■ _____
    - ■ _____
  - ○ _____
    - ■ _____
    - ■ _____
    - ■ _____
  - ○ _____
    - ■ _____

- ■ _____
- ■ _____

- • [SECTION #4] _____
  - ○ _____
    - ■ _____
    - ■ _____
    - ■ _____
  - ○ _____
    - ■ _____
    - ■ _____
    - ■ _____
  - ○ _____
    - ■ _____
    - ■ _____
    - ■ _____
  - ○ _____
    - ■ _____
    - ■ _____
    - ■ _____

- • [SECTION #5] _____
  - ○ _____
    - ■ _____
    - ■ _____
    - ■ _____
  - ○ _____

151

- ■ _____
- ■ _____
- ■ _____
- ○ _____
- ■ _____
- ■ _____
- ■ _____
- ○ _____
- ■ _____
- ■ _____
- ■ _____

- • [SECTION #6] _____
  - ○ _____
    - ■ _____
    - ■ _____
    - ■ _____
  - ○ _____
    - ■ _____
    - ■ _____
    - ■ _____
  - ○ _____
    - ■ _____
    - ■ _____
    - ■ _____
  - ○ _____
    - ■ _____

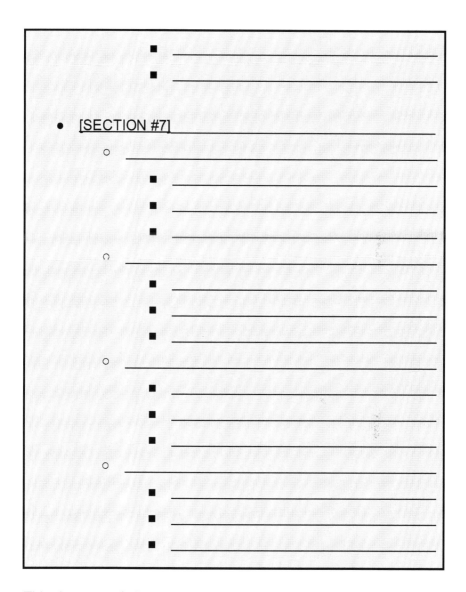

- [SECTION #7]

This is one of the most important, if not the most important, exercises in this book.

Hence, make sure you have spent the time completing this exercise as it WILL make writing your book 10X times easier.

Let's continue..

#4) SECTION BRANDING & #5) CHAPTER BRANDING

That's right, I'm just going to bundle them together for you.

Every section, and every chapter, needs a great title.

Now, these titles are nowhere near as important as your book title, and do not deserve as much of your time, however, they are still very important.

Each section, and each chapter, is it's own brand.

The best example I can come up with to explain how this works is the Coca Cola brand.

The name of the company is The Coca Cola Company.

Within that company, they have various other brands... Coca Cola, Sprite, Fanta, Vitamin Water, etc.

Those are all brands underneath the over-riding brand of The Coca Cola Company.

Now, those brands (Coca Cola, Sprite, Fanta)... they also have brands within them.

For example, the Sprite brand has multiple brands within it... Sprite Zero, Sprite Cranberry, etc

Here's how it looks in a different format:

- The Coca Cola Company
    - Coca Cola
        - Coca Cola Zero
        - Diet Coke
        - Coca Cola Light

- Sprite
  - Sprite Zero
  - Sprite Cranberry
- Fanta
  - Fanta Zero
  - Fanta Orange
- Vitamin Water
  - Vitamin Water Power-C
  - Vitamin Water Essential
  - Vitamin Water Restore

The Coca Cola Company... that like your book brand *(your book title)*

Coca Cola, Sprite, Fanta… these are like your section brands *(the titles of your sections)*

Sprite Zero, Sprite Cranberry… these are like your chapter brands *(the titles of your chapters)*

See how it works?

The keys to creating great section, and chapter, titles are pretty much the same as the keys for creating great book titles.

The same principles apply.

The objective of each section, or chapter, title is to grab the attention of the reader and get them to read that section, or chapter.

Make sure you keep that in mind.

Oh… and you don't have to spend nearly as much time on these titles as you do on your *book title*.

So, right now, take 10 minutes and title all of your sections, and all of your chapters.

```
┌─────────────────────────────────────────────────────┐
│           SECTION & CHAPTER BRANDING:                 │
│                                                       │
│   •  [SECTION #1]_____        │
│          ○    _____        │
│          ○    _____        │
│          ○    _____        │
│          ○    _____        │
│                                                       │
│   •  [SECTION #2]_____        │
│          ○    _____        │
│          ○    _____        │
│          ○    _____        │
│          ○    _____        │
│                                                       │
│   •  [SECTION #3]_____        │
│          ○    _____        │
│          ○    _____        │
│          ○    _____        │
│          ○    _____        │
│                                                       │
│   •  [SECTION #4]_____        │
│          ○    _____        │
│          ○    _____        │
│          ○    _____        │
│          ○    _____        │
│                                                       │
│   •  [SECTION #5]_____        │
│          ○    _____        │
└─────────────────────────────────────────────────────┘
```

- ○ _____
- ○ _____
- ○ _____
- **[SECTION #6]** _____
  - ○ _____
  - ○ _____
  - ○ _____
  - ○ _____
- **[SECTION #7]** _____
  - ○ _____
  - ○ _____
  - ○ _____
  - ○ _____

And *viola*.

Great job. You now have an entire writing game plan for your book.

Congratulations on getting to this point.

In the next chapter, we are going to go into your design.

Your front cover, your back cover, your book spine; how can you get them all designed quickly (and effectively!)

You're on the right track.

Let's continue..

CHAPTER 14: CREATING YOUR AUDIENCE-CAPTIVATING DESIGN

The Burj Khalifa… The Eiffel Tower… The Statue Of Liberty…

..what is it, above all else, that makes these buildings stand out, attract tourists, and be exceptional?

I would say it's..

..the unique, audience-captivating designs.

Seriously, if the Burj Khalifa look like every other skyscraper, hundreds, and thousands, of people wouldn't flock to see it every single week.

Unique, cutting edge, audience-captivating design.

Now, if your book cover looks exactly like every other cover in your market, that won't really help your book sales.

Mundane, repetitive, boring design doesn't attract audiences.

This chapter consists of 4 main parts..

In fact, here's the checklist for this section:

- FRONT COVER DESIGN
- BACK COVER DESIGN
- SPINE DESIGN
- FINALIZED PRINT-READY DESIGN

Here's the thing, I just spent the last few sentences talking about creating a unique, audience-captivating design..

..hence, what I'm about to say may shock *(and even confuse)* you a little..

You really?

Here goes..

When it comes to book cover design, pretty much every design idea you will ever have has already been done in some way or another..

You may think that that is bad news.. *it's not.*

It's really not.

It's actually great news *(and here's why..)*

Remember the quote I quoted earlier in this book..

'*Success leaves clues*' - *Anthony Robbins*

Well… if every great design idea has already been tested, then that means you already have the data you need to make intelligent and effective design decisions.

159

Yes, you hold the power.

Based on everything I have just said, the next logical step is for you to create, what I call, your *BOOK COVER SWIPE FILE.*

Which sounds fancy, but it's really just a collection of book covers *(front, back and spine)* that you like, and have seen get great results before *(covers that you can model for your design)*

So, right now, take 5 minutes, search your bookshelf, or an online bookstore, and find at least 10 FRONT covers that you like, have seen work effectively, and that you can model for your book cover.

Stop reading for a moment and complete that exercise. Go.

Great. Now, do the same for BACK covers.

Stop reading again and find back covers that you like and can model and add them to your *book cover swipe file.*

Now, lastly, repeat that process one final time. This time save the images of 10 book SPINES *(side covers)* that you like, and can model. Complete this exercise now… and go.

Congrats, you now have your very own *book cover swipe file.*

Your goal is to constantly grow this swipe file as you write more and more books (see you I **didn't** say 'if you write more books')

Now, your goal is to essentially hand pick elements from those covers *(the ones in your book cover swipe file)* that you think could work on your book covers, and test.

Test that fonts. Test that styles. Test images.

Test. Test. Test.

However, before you dive into the cover design process, you must know that there are 3 main methods of cover design.

Let's go through these 3 main methods:

1. DO IT YOURSELF

There are many different tools, and pieces of software, you can use to very affordably get your book cover created. This is the cheapest, yet most time-consuming option.

Also, depending on your level of skills, this is either the option that will make your book cover look the best, or the worst.

That's the first method. Plain and simple; *do it yourself.*

2. FREELANCERS

There are many, many sites where you can get your front cover, back cover, and spine designed to a very high standard, in just a few days, for less than $100.

However, times change.

Technology changes.

Hence, if you want the most up-to-date list of tools for freelancing and cover design, simply go to the free bonuses page for this book now:

FreeBonuses.6DayPublish.com

This free bonuses page is designed to save you many hours, days, and maybe even weeks, of searching and testing… we have tested many of the tools for you, and we can help you save your valuable time by simply giving a list of the tools that have worked to you

Hence, that's what we did with this free bonuses page.

3. AGENCY

This is the most expensive method, however, it's also the method that, most of the time, will give you the best quality cover design.

There you have it... those are the 3 main methods for getting your cover designed.

Now, let's go through exactly what you need to design:

#1) FRONT COVER DESIGN

This is, without a doubt, the most piece of design you will need to do for your book.

Your front cover is like your first impression... and we all know that if we make the wrong first impression, it's a heck of a lot harder to change someone's opinion of you afterwards.

The same applies to your cover design; make a good first impression.

Here are the key elements that your front cover should consist of:

- BOOK TITLE (duh!)
- BOOK SUBTITLE
- AUTHOR NAME
- AUTHOR CREDITS (OPTIONAL)
- IMAGE/IMAGES (OPTIONAL)
- COLOUR

Now, if you have done the first 4 exercises in this stage of the 6 Day Publish Process, meeting that 6 step criteria should be a piece of cake.. a complete walk in the park.

But remember, make sure you use your *book cover swipe file* to help you identify the most effective things to put on your cover *(plus, where, and how, to put them)*

After your front cover design, you have the next step..

#2) BACK COVER DESIGN

Imagine you are in an elevator going from floor 1 to floor 28.

You have about 30 seconds before the elevator reaches your floor.

You are in the elevator with the ideal prospect for your book.

They just asked you about your book… they showed some interest.

You have 30 seconds to sell a copy of your book; that's the objective at least.

What do you say?

What do you tell this prospect?

Really think about this.

That's what your back cover is… it's like an elevator pitch for your book.

Now, if you choose, you can refer back to the *BUYING HOOK ANALYSIS* exercise in stage 2; **pre-work.**

In fact, if you completed that exercise correctly, you can just use exactly what you wrote in that exercise for your back cover text.

Or, you can modify and refine what you wrote before.

It's all up to you, it's your book **:)**

Let me break down exactly what you need for your back cover text..

Here's the back cover text for this book:

> *TURN YOUR IDEA INTO A PUBLISHED BOOK IN 6 DAYS, OR LESS!*

That was the first part... *your back cover headline...* designed to grab attention (you can use *your disruptive idea* for this.)

> *Do you have a message to share, a difference to make, or a business to grow?*
>
> *Do you want to multiply your credibility, skyrocket your influence, or just plain and simple, make more money?*

That was the second part... two enrolling questions crafted to get a **'YES'** response, and gain buy in from your readers.. *(read: you)*

> *For weeks, months (and maybe even years) you have been told that the secret to marketing your business, gaining celebrity status, sharing your message and multiplying your income is publishing your own book.*
>
> *And frankly, it's all true.*

Third part... listing benefits and sharing about the importance of the topic (book creation).

> *However, maybe you have thought to yourself, 'I don't know where to start, it all sounds too complicated,' or simply, 'It just takes too long'*

In 6 Day Publish, Bogdan Juncewicz reveals a game-changing new system for turning an idea into a published book in 6 days, or less.

Fourth part… sharing the benefits and talking about what makes your book different from all the others *(the differentiation)*

Bogdan Juncewicz has spent the last 5 years learning with, learning from and, most importantly, teaching thousands and thousands of students all around the world, across multiple continents, elite-level business and life strategies. Bogdan published his first book, Skilled Success, at age 17, and is the CEO of 2 digital businesses.

Fifth part… what makes you credible to teach this topic? Why should your target prospects want to learn from you? In this part, I *(and you should too)* share what makes me a credible expert able to teach this particular topic.

The goal of this book is simple: to share with you EVERYTHING you need to know to turn your idea into a professionally-written, full-length, published book in 6 days, or less!

Sixth part… Answering possible objections… *'professionally written, full-length'*… and restating the key benefit *(the disruptive idea.)*

You can follow that template if you choose.

Your back cover has a few key criteria:

- HEADLINE
- BOOK COVER TEXT
- COLOUR
- IMAGE *(OPTIONAL)*
- BOOK DETAILS (BARCODE, ISBN NUMBER/S, ETC)

Once again, and I can't say this enough..

Do not attempt to recreate the wheel..

..find what works, model it.

Test and improve.

Next, and this one is short and sweet..

#3) OΓINE DEOION

I'm not talking about the spine that holds your body in balance..

..I'm talking about the side cover of your book *(your book spine.)*

Now, I won't spend much time on this because there's not really much to spend time on.

A book spine.

You need one.

Here are the 4 criteria for a book spine:

- BOOK TITLE
- SUBTITLE *(IF YOU CAN FIT IT IN - OPTIONAL)*
- AUTHOR NAME
- COLOUR

That's it. Plain and simple.

Model the book spines in your *book cover swipe file*.

And last, but not least..

#4) FINALIZED PRINT-READY DESIGN

This step really differs depends on what publishing method *(or which publisher)* you are planning to use for your book.

In most cases, this step is where you turn your book cover pieces *(front cover, back cover, book spine)* into a PDF file that follows this format:

BACK COVER DESIGN	SPINE	FRONT COVER DESIGN

All together as one PDF file.

Sizing depends on the size you want to publish your book in.

The standard book size is 6" by 9".

Then you take that PDF, upload it *(or send it to your publisher)*..

..and *voila!* Your design is complete **:)**

That's what this step is... plain and simple, turn your 3 cover images into one pdf file ready for publishing.

So, right now, take the time, pick which one of the 3 design methods you want to go with, and start designing.

Once you have either, outsourced the work to a freelancer, outsourced it to an agency, or you have created your own design, come back to this page and let's continue.

And in case you're wondering..

No, you don't have to have a fully completed design before you get into stage 4 *(stage 4; actually writing the damn thing.)*

When I have book covers designed, I outsource the design work, I share all the design instructions, share everything they need to know to get it designed, and I continue with the 6 Day Publish Process while the design is being completed for me.

So there you have it.

We started with stage 1; **pre-work,** and identified why you are actually writing your book, and the purpose it plays in the overall scheme of things..

..and now we have gone through, and completed stage 3; **present**.

3 stages down.

Just 2 stages to go.

Right now, everything is in place for you to get started with stage 4; *produce (a.k.a... the stage where you actually start writing)*

Before we continue, here are approximations to share how long each stage in the 6 Day Publish Process should take..

STAGE	TIME TO COMPLETE
STAGE 1: PREPARE	1 - 3 HOURS (+ Years of life study)
STAGE 2: PRE-WORK	2 - 5 HOURS
STAGE 3: PRESENT	3 - 7 HOURS (Depending on method)
STAGE 4: PRODUCE	25 - 40 HOURS
STAGE 5: PUBLISH	DEPENDS*

*DEPENDS: With CreateSpace, the Amazon self-publishing company, it takes 1 - 2 HOURS. Other methods differ. Differ, a lot.

In the next section, we are going to dive into stage 4; *produce*..

..you have everything else pretty much handled, now, *how do you turn it all into a 150 - 250 page book that readers, buy, love, and tell all their friends about?*

How do you get your book actually written?

That's what we are going to cover in the next section.

You've done phenomenal so far *(if you been doing the exercises that is. Yes, I'm watching you)..*

It's time to turn it all into a masterpiece that you will look back on, years from now, with complete gratitude and appreciation.

It's time to write..

SECTION 7:

STAGE 4: PRODUCE

CHAPTER 15: WRITING IS THE SECRET

You have arrived..

..at that moment..

..at that point..

..when it's time to turn all of your preparation, and all of your brilliance, into written words that will change lives.

'The secret to writing a book is writing'

Writing is the secret.

As flat out simplistic and obvious as that is, so many people miss that one key; *writing.*

They think about writing a book, they talk about writing a book, they commit to writing a book, they sit down to start writing a book…

..yet they don't actually… you know… start writing.

Frankly, this stage *(this section)* should be the longest and most complex because it's the stage that we, as authors, spend the most on..

..however it's not.

In fact, if you have read all of the sections leading up to this one, you already know everything you need to know to get your book written.

You could just skip this section.

Don't. *(because each section is important)*

But, you could and you would still get the results you want.

Anyway, here are the key elements of a book you have to create.

You can find examples of most of these in this book:

- TITLE PAGE
- COPYRIGHT NOTICE *(OPTIONAL)*
- DEDICATION *(OPTIONAL)*
- ACKNOWLEDGEMENTS *(OPTIONAL)*
- TABLE OF CONTENTS
- THE SECTIONS & CHAPTERS
- OTHER PROMOTIONAL STUFF (OPTIONAL)

So, how to write a book?

Simply follow the book structure you created in stage 3; ***present.***

So, without further ado, stop reading and start writing.

CHAPTER 16: WRITING HACKS

We live in a world now where the average attention span is… oh, look… new Facebook message..

..look, new app notification.

In fact, let me go a step further..

According to scientists, smartphones have left humans with a shorter attention span than goldfish.

Results of recent studies show the average human attention span has fallen from 12 seconds in 2000, or around the time the mobile revolution began, to eight seconds now.

Goldfish, meanwhile, are believed to have an attention span of nine seconds.

Yes, we, as human beings, have a shorter attention span than goldfish.

Shocking, huh?

Now that you know that though, it may change how you look at writing.

The goal of a book is for people to actually read it, right?

If that's the goal.. the purpose.. of your book, then you may want to restructure how you write *(just like I did)*

I don't know about you, but if I look down at a page with size 6 font, huge blocks of non-stop content, no spacing..

..my mind just switches off.

That's why this book is written the way it's written.

Short lines.

Lots of spacing.

It's written in this way because I understand human attention.

I understand that if you write like your English teacher told you to, you will lose most of your readers.

And you'll lose them for good.

Now, you don't have to write in the writing structure I do, it's all up to you.

It's your book.

What I will say though is that, based on my experience with book writing, copywriting and digital marketing, this style of writing is purposely optimised for engagement.

And based on the fact that you are reading these words, it works.

So, ask yourself... *what writing style am I going to use, and how does this affect my outcomes?*

Great.. before your attention span moves onto thinking about something else.. let me share about one more so-called writing hack...

This writing hack is all about **writing personality**.

You see, I love reading.

It's not uncommon for me to get on a flight and read 1-2 books by the time that flight lands.

And if I look back at the books that I have really connect to, a lot of it comes down to this..

This makes the difference in sales, in marketing, in business, in book creation, and in pretty much everything else.

The key; **Writing Personality.**

You want to write with the intention of actually connecting with your readers.

A book isn't simply about content delivery anymore, it's about more than that.

A book is also a golden opportunity for you to connect with, build trust with and build rapport with your readers.

You want to share stories with your readers.

You want to share your life experiences with your readers.

You want to make each reader feel like you are talking just to them… like a conversation.

Now, this doesn't always apply.

If you're writing a book where your target market is banking executives, this doesn't apply anywhere near as much *(it does still apply though…)*

It's all about communicating to your audience in a way that provides value, provides engagement and builds connection.

And the absolute best way to do all of this is to be real with your audience.

There is so much hype out there that your audience sees, you need to become the breath of fresh air; you need to build trust and build relationship with your audience.

If you apply these two writing hacks; writing structuring and writing personality, you will have a huge advantage over the competition.

With that said, the best way to optimise what works is to actually write it, then optimise it afterwards.

Anyhoo..

This stage; **produce**, is made up of two main parts…

1. WRITING
2. FORMATING/OPTIMIZING

After you write your book *(and only once you finish writing your book)* your role is to then re-read your book multiple times, format it, improve it and make tweaks before finally moving onto the last heavenly stage; **publish**.

With that said, don't over-do the formating.

Remember the chapter about *'the perfection myth..?'*

The content in that chapter applies to formating/optimizing above all else.

Anyhoo, I have good news for you..

..right now, in this moment, you have EVERYTHING you need to know about book creation to get your book written and ready to publish.

The secret to writing a book is to write…

..it's time for you to begin..

SECTION 8:

STAGE 5: PUBLISH

CHAPTER 17: THE FINISH LINE

You can see it in front of you…

…you have arrived at that point when all of the hard work pays off.

Imagine that you have just ran 41.5km…

..and in just a few hundred metres you will reach the finish line and complete the marathon.

That's what this stage is like.

If you on this stage you have done the hard work..

..you have done the heavy lifting..

..and now it's time to get your book published.

With book publishing you really have two main options:

1. PUBLISH THROUGH A PUBLISHER
2. SELF-PUBLISHING

Frankly, I can't teach you about publishing through a publisher at the time of writing this book because that isn't where my expertise lies.

My expertise lies in getting books self-published FAST, and then launching those books to the public through digital marketing strategies I use everyday in my digital businesses.

The matter of the fact is that you can get your book published, printed and ready-to-sell very, very quickly by self-publishing it through the right platforms.

Imagine if just 24 hours after writing your book you could have your book listed for sale in the world's largest bookstore..

Imagine if you could reach potentially hundreds of thousands of people with your book just hours after you get your book published..

It's all possible with **self-publishing.**

And imagine if you could sell thousands and even millions of copies, and you never had to have a single book in inventory in your life (and you never had to physically ship a copy by yourself... ever...)

Also possible with something called **print-on-demand.**

Here's the thing, the self-publishing tools change constantly, so instead of me listing the best tools here in this book, you can find all of the best tools and in-depth guides on how to get your book published by going here:

FreeBonuses.6DayPublish.com

See how that works...

Inside your book, to keep your book up-to-date you want to avoid listing current trends, current best solutions, etc, as much as you can… as much as possible.

Anyhoo, if you have gone through the previous 4 stages in this 6 Day Publish Process then this last stage should be a piece of cake.

In the next section, I am going to share how you can get supported along your book publishing journey for even better results…

Also, I will reveal two more powerful writing hacks that may just change how you write forever.

Pretty big buildup, huh?

Let's see if it worked..

Continue to the next page, and let's continue..

SECTION 9:

THE NEXT STEPS

CHAPTER 18: YOU'RE NOT ALONE

His story was amazing…

..very inspiring.

What seems like a while back now, I spent a few hours at an evening event learning from a guy by the name of Leon Taylor.

Chances are, you have no idea who he is.

I didn't either *(until I heard him speak.)*

He's actually a Olympic medalist *(he won a silver medal for diving)*

You can search him up if you want.

Getting off point here..

He was sharing about his story.

About his journey to the Olympics.

All the up's and all the downs. *(it was a great story btw)*

He then continued to talk about a kid he used to mentor (and still mentors)..

A kid by the name of..

Tom Daley

If you don't know who Tom Daley is... he is one of the youngest and most successful divers in the UK *(and the world!)*

We became the FINA Diving World Champion at age 15.

(Yeah, age 15!! Damn!)

Anyhoo.. he went on to talk about the #1 main thing that accelerated his (and Tom Daley's) success so radically..

'What was it?..' you may think..

Personal mentoring.

(in other words, *personal coaching*)

So many successful people have mentors. Have coaches.

Whether it's Mark Zuckerberg's mentor/coach (Steve Jobs)..

..or Oprah Winfrey mentor/coach (Maya Angelou)

..or Tony Robbin's mentor (Jim Rohn)..

Many, many successful people have, or have had, mentors/coaches that support them to achieve results.

Why would anyone attempt to figure everything out by themselves when they could bypass those years of trial and error through coaching, right..?

Personally, I don't get it.

In the words of Tony Robbins...
'Success leaves clues'

Hence, I ask you..

Do you want to turn your idea into a published book in 6 days, or less?

If you reading these words, chances are, that's a yes.

And btw, congratulations on getting to this point *(I'll talk more about this later)*

So, if you want to turn your idea into a published book in 6 days, or less, the fastest way for you to do that *(other than actually applying the stuff in this book)* is to get someone who has been there and done that to support you to get there.

You see, I don't want this book to be something that people just read, put down and treat like any other book.

That's not the business I want to be in.

I much prefer to do *everything* in my power to help people actually apply the stuff in this book for their idea, and for their situation, so that they get results... so that they actually get their books written and published, fast!

I want to help you turn your idea into a published book, fast!

That's why I decided to offer you this special bonus; **a free 30 minute book strategy session** during which I will personally guide you through this entire book process.

During these 30 minutes I will get on the phone with you and personally walk you through the stages of the 6 Day Publish Process for YOUR idea and YOUR book.

I will answer all of your questions and help you supercharge your book results.

How many insights, and learnings, can you accumulate by personally working with a 2 time speed author, international speaker and CEO of 2 digital businesses?

Claim your free 30 minute book strategy session now:

FreeStrategySession.6DayPublish.com

It's no coincidence that the world's highest achieving people... top athletes, top business people, top investors, have coaches to support them.

And you too, do want to get the best possible results, in the fastest possible way, don't you?

If your answer is YES, then this free 30 minute strategy session is for you.

You see, I do not offer this free 30 minute strategy session to anyone and everyone...

..because frankly, not everyone is ready for it.

This free 30 minute strategy session is reserved for people who have gone ahead and gotten their copy of this book. It's for people that has shown that they are interested and committed.

With that said, it's completely optional…

..and if you don't want to supercharge your book creation results, please do yourself (and me) a favour and save our time.

If you DO want to supercharge your book creation results though, then go here and claim your free 30 minute book strategy session now:

FreeStrategySession.6DayPublish.com

Imagine if you could have me personally guide you through the process and supercharge your book results..

Imagine if you could have all of your book questions answered.. if you could gain even greater clarity to move forward with..

That's what this 30 minute strategy session will give you.

With that said, this free bonus offer came disappear at anytime, and you risk losing out *(it may have even disappeared already)*... hence, if you want to supercharge your book results through powerful, personalized and free coaching, you must act now:

FreeStrategySession.6DayPublish.com

Now, I really need you to get this, this strategy session is simply an accelerator and amplifier of results.

The information in this book, applied, will get you better book results than you can ever imagine.

Ok, so before we continue, I want to thank you.

Thank you and congratulations on getting to this point in the book. It shows me a lot about you.

A lot of people (82% of american adults reportedly) want to write a book, but you are the one who stepped it up and took a huge leap forward to making that dream a reality.

And as I said before, it's your obligation to get your book completed and published.

That's the belief I live my life with. If you have a message that will help people live a happier, more successful and more fulfilling life, it's you duty to do everything in your power to share that message with the world.

Your book will become your secret weapon… a weapon that over time moves you up to near-celebrity status, opens up a flood of amazing life opportunities and helps you grow your business, career and life results exponentially.

In the next, and final, chapter I will share the final piece that you need to get started making rapid and powerful progress on your book.

What you will discover in the final chapter will help you start reaping rewards from your book before you even start writing it, and it will give you a huge dose of constant motivation to get your book written and published.

It's one simple, powerful strategy that you can implement TODAY to accelerate your book progress rapidly and start reaping book rewards starting today..

The final chapter awaits..

CHAPTER 19: THE FINAL PUZZLE PIECE

Woah!

It sure has been an incredible adventure we have been on together over the course of this book, hasn't it?

We have covered a lot. (And I mean… A LOT!)

Let's quickly summarize before we continue with this chapter…

You started reading this book, probably a little, if not very, curious about what this crazy 17 year old kid is talking about…

Yes, 99% of your mind may have believed, or at least been hopeful, that turning an idea into a published book in 6 days, or less is possible, but maybe that 1% of your mind remained skeptical.

And maybe you mind is still a little skeptical that it's even possible.

That's fine.

That will change when you actually make it happen *(and you will make it happen!)*

You started diving into the sections of this book.. with each section.. with each chapter, serving a different purpose..

..yet all serving the same goal..

..to give you everything you need to know to turn your idea into a professionally-written, published, ready-to-sell book in 6 days (or oven loool)

> **Section 1:** A book. It's more than just a book. It's the ultimate thousand year old marketing tool.
>
> Boosted credibility. More business. Expert positioning. Your book can give you all of that (and more!)

The framework for your book success was laid, and it was time to dig into the action plan.. Into the proven strategies that get results.

> **Section 2:** *What is it that holds so many back from turning their ideas into published books?*
>
> What are the myths that so many buy into that limit their potential… and more importantly, how can you avoid these common pitfalls, so that you can share your message and make a difference with your published book.
>
> *The slow and steady myth.*
>
> *The perfection myth.*
>
> *The jump straight in myth.*
>
> Enough is enough. You won't fall victim to these any longer.

It's time for you to get your book written, and published.. and get it done fast.

I believe that we, people on this planet, the human race, are only tapping into a fraction of our true potential, and I believe there is so much untapped potential in people waiting to be uncovered.

I have made it my mission to help people tap into this potential, because I believe that we all, deep down, want to be able to look back at our lives with joy, gratitude and pride.

Hence, from when I was about 15, until the time of my inevitable death... I will do everything in my power, every single day, to share this message of potential, accelerated achievement and transformation. It's my mission, my duty to do so... this is why I am on this planet.

This book is more than just a book about writing books, this book is a book about purpose... what message, what content, what difference do you want to be the messenger for on this planet...?

> **Section 3:** Within this section, I started sharing about this incredible 6 Day Publish Process... the process that will help you turn ideas into published books effectively, over and over again.
>
> *Yes, turning an idea into a published book in 6 days, or less, it sure does sound like a great idea, but HOW exactly do I make that happen?*
>
> Within this section, I revealed the 6 Day Publish Checklist and shared about the 5 core stages of book creation.
>
> **Prepare. Pre-work. Present. Produce. Publish.**

A proven 5 stage process for turning an idea into a published book.

After that, we started digging deeper into each of these 5 stages…

I believe that if we want to achieve success at anything, we just need to find people who have achieved what we want to achieve, and we need to model their success.

Study their success. Study what made them succeed. And model it.

And that's exactly what you're doing with The 6 Day Publish Process, your modeling the success of someone who has been there and achieve the results already (yours truly). Congratulations.

Section 4: Within this section we covered stage 1 of the 6 Day Publish Process; **prepare**.

How can you discover exactly what your target customers will respond to before you even write your first word?

What already influences your target market, and how can you use the preparation strategies revealed in this section to get the best book results possible?

In this section, you started getting your hands dirty as you started putting in the work for YOUR book.

As I have banged on about… this isn't a book you read.

It's a book you DO.

With each section in this book you immersed yourself deeper in the 6 Day Publish Process… digging deeper and deeper into this proven system for turning an idea into a published book in 6 days, or less.

Section 5: This section; **pre-work.**

What is the purpose of your book?

What's your disruptive idea?

Within this section, we dug deep into the purpose of your book. As you already know, the clearer you are on your book purpose, the better your book will be.

Clarity leads to power.

Then we moved from pre-work to the next stage in the 6 Day Publish Process..

Section 6: Present; people DO judge a book by the cover.

Hence, what is that makes a book cover attention-grabbing and audience-captivating?

Within this section, we also talked about your book overview… which is arguably the most important pre-writing document you will create for your book.

'Give me boundaries, so I can be free'

It's all about setting up a framework for your success. Then executing to get results.

I wholeheartedly believe that it's the action-takers that make incredible stuff happen on this planet.

People say that it's the dreamers that make things happen. I don't buy into that theory.

I believe that anyone can have a dream, anyone can create a plan, anyone can talk about achieving incredible thing..

..yet, few execute. Few take action, and few make the world a better place for everyone else on this incredible planet.

I believe in action.

> **Section 7:** Within this stage, we talked about exactly that... taking action. Executing. ***Stage 4: Produce.*** Writing is the secret to writing a book..
>
> So many people think about writing a book.. talk about writing a book... schedule time to write a book... plan writing a book... sit down to write a book..
>
> ..but few actually complete what they start and actually write their book.
>
> Yet, it's this minority that truly get incredible results.
>
> And I know that you are part of that group - the group of action-takers.
>
> The fact that you are reading these words shows me that, it shows me you are an action taker.
>
> And, as I said, it's the action takers in this world that make incredible things happen. It's the action takers who get their books written and published for the world to see.
>
> *And you do want to get your book written and published, don't you?*

Once you have followed through the first 4 stages, we concluded with stage 5.. the easy part.

> **Section 8:** Within this section, we covered the final stage in the 6 Day Publish Process; **publish.**
>
> The dessert within the book creation meal.
>
> The point that all the hard work comes to… the finish line… the moment when you become a published author and can start reaping all the rewards that come with that title.
>
> Stage 5 in the 6 Day Publish Process; **publish**.

And that brings us to here.

To right here… section 9.

It brings us to these words… the words you are reading right now.

To this moment in time.

Thank you for your trust and attention.

And, congratulations on your commitment to get to this point.

However, this book is not the end.

Far from it.

This book is simply the beginning.

Now it's time for you to take everything you have learned within this book, and apply it to your life to get the results you want.

The goal of this book is for it to support you long after you finish reading it.

The 6 Day Publish Checklist and all of the exercises in this book are repeatable.

It's a system; it works to produce the same great results over and over again.

You put in an idea, you go through the start-to-finish process laid out in this book, and out comes an incrodiblo now book.

Ok, now before I let you go, let me share one more powerful thing that will allow you to reap the rewards of being a published author before you even write the first word of your book.

Plus, this will give you huge doses of consistent motivation to go through this 6 Day Publish Process.

Here's the strategy...

Declare Yourself An Author Now

That's right. If you have done the exercises in this book you should already have a brand name for your book, and that's all you need to start tapping into the power of this strategy.

Once you have the brand name (the title) for your upcoming book, start calling yourself an author. It's kinda like..

Yes, I'm Bogdan, author of the upcoming new book; *6 Day Publish*..

I'm [YOUR NAME], author of the upcoming new book; [BOOK TITLE]

This exercise has huge power...

Complete this exercise now..

DECLARE YOURSELF AN AUTHOR NOW:

I'm _____, and I'm the author of the

upcoming new book _____.

This is powerful for two reasons:

1. You start reaping some of the rewards straight away, meaning you can start gaining interest and credibility for, and from, your upcoming book before it's even written.. *(emphasis on the word 'some.')*

2. It gives you public accountability to get your book written and published, especially once you hear people excited about your upcoming book.

There you have it. Right now you are an upcoming author of your new book, and after you follow through the 6 Day Publish Process laid out in this book, you will become a published author of your new book.

It has been a pleasure, and a privilege, to share everything in this book with you.

This brings a huge smile to my face every time I think about it. However, as I said before, this is my duty, it's my obligation to serve you, and others around the world, to live a better life.
I guess this adventure is coming to end... for now at least.

I want to leave you with this...

You have life experiences, you have life stories, you have messages that can change the lives of people on this incredible planet.

Your experiences, your stories, your thoughts are far more valuable than you can ever imagine; you can *be a messenger for change.*

I believe that you and I, we can inspire millions of people on this planet. It's only once you step into this belief that you will truly make your difference on this planet.

Everyday, wake up as that messenger for change, and inspire those around you, inspire strangers you are yet to meet, inspire the people around you, and inspire humanity to step up to their greatness.

We, people on this planet, are not insignificant.

You are not insignificant.

You have the power to make a difference.

You have the power to change lives of people on this planet.

You have the power!

It's time for you to unleash it to inspire the world in you incredible way; *be a messenger for change.*

Till next time,
Bogdan Juncewicz

I want to thank you for your trust and attention. Go and live your dreams; *be a messenger for change.*

DEDICATION

I dedicate this book to the people, and the communities, around me that have supported me on my journey.

To the people I have learned with, trained with, upskilled with and experienced incredible adventures with.

To those who have been there for me during my biggest failures, and have been there to support me, no matter what.

To those who have pushed me to higher and higher levels of commitment, determination and success.

To all the people I call family. Thank you.

BOOK CREATION & PUBLISH CHECKLIST

DOCUMENT	COMPLETE?
PREPARE	
- READ & SUMMARIZE 5 SIMILAR BOOKS	
- SUMMARIZE 5 MOST SIMILAR COURSES/EVENTS/VIDEOS	
- WRITE LIST OF EVERYTHING I ALREADY KNOW ON GIVEN TOPIC	
- RESEARCH COMPETITION	
PRE-WORK	
- MARKET PROBLEM ANALYSIS	
- BUYER CUSTOMER AVATAR	
- DIFFERENTIATION FACTOR ANALYSIS	
- DISRUPTIVE IDEA ANALYSIS	
- BUYING HOOK ANALYSIS	
- EDUCATIONAL PURPOSE	
- COMMERCIAL PURPOSE	
- MARKETING & PROFIT STRATEGY ANALYSIS	
- PUBLISHING STRATEGY	
PRESENT	
- BOOK TITLE	
- BOOK SUBTITLE/S	
- COLOUR PREFERENCES AND ANALYSIS	
- AUTHOR + AUTHOR CREDITS	
- SECTION OVERVIEW (Usually 3-9)	
- SECTION CHAPTER OVERVIEW (Usually 10 - 30)	
- CHAPTER KEY POINT OVERVIEW (Usually 3-8/chapter)	
- SECTION BRANDING	
- CHAPTER BRANDING	
- FRONT COVER DESIGN	
- BACK COVER DESIGN	
- SPINE DESIGN	
- FINALIZED PRINT-READY DESIGN	

PRODUCE

- INTERIOR TITLE PAGE
- COPYRIGHT NOTICE (OPTIONAL)
- DEDICATION (OPTIONAL)
- ACKNOWLEDGEMENTS (OPTIONAL)
- TABLE OF CONTENTS
- SECTION #1 WRITTEN
- SECTION #2 WRITTEN
- SECTION #3 WRITTEN
- SECTION #4 WRITTEN
- SECTION #5 WRITTEN
- SECTION #6 WRITTEN
- SECTION #7 WRITTEN
- SECTION #8 WRITTEN
- SECTION #9 WRITTEN

- BASIC BOOK FORMATING CHECK (SPELL, GRAMMAR CHECK)
- TITLES, TABLE OF CONTENTS, SECTIONS & CHAPTERS FORMAT
- JUSTIFICATION & CENTRALIZATION FORMAT
- BOLD/ITALICS/UNDERLINE FORMAT
- FORMAT KEY SOUNDBITES TO STAND OUT
- FINALIZED PRINT-READY PDF

PUBLISH

- REVIEW/BOOK PROOFING
- RETAIL PRICING
- HIT 'PUBLISH'

Printed in Great Britain
by Amazon